GIRLS™

Girls Initiating Real Living Standards

CHANGE YOUR VIEW, CHANGE YOUR WORLD
Planting empowerment seeds to grow a life of success!

by
Deirdre Skelton

D1089416

DISCLAIMER:

This **G.I.R.L.S.** curriculum is a strategic, layered, common sense, standards-based curriculum. It builds upon each concept presented in the previous lesson, in order to build a solid foundation upon which to develop a real living standard.

The order of the lessons is important because each concept builds upon the preceding one, so that a solid sense of who you are, whose you are, and what your standards are will be constructed.
The activities included in this curriculum are samples and are in no way exhaustive. There are many activities available – in workbooks, on the internet, on inspirational sites, etc. that can be used to instill the lessons.

The curriculum is consistent with other researched based girl empowerment data.

Copyright © by Deirdre Skelton 2022

G.I.R.L.S. (Girls Initiating Real Living Standards) Change Your View, Change Your World
Planting Empowerment Seeds to Grow A Life of Success! ™ *All* rights reserved. No part of this book may be reproduced, stored in a retrieval system, or transmitted in any form or by any means, electronic, mechanical, photocopying, recording or otherwise without expressed permission of the author, except for brief quotations for critical reviews.

Permission is granted for individuals, parents, teachers, and group leaders to photocopy the pages included in the exercises that indicate they should be photocopied for personal, home, classroom, or group work only.

DEDICATION

I dedicate this book to my parents,
William A. Skelton, Sr. and Annamary Henderson Skelton.
You not only told all your children
– Billy, Michael, Deirdre, Annamaria and Gloria –
that we were loved, important, and valued,
you showed us by pouring your time, money, and energy into us.
Your investment produced five upstanding citizens
who never had an encounter with the law, five homeowners, and
four college graduates. We knew who we were, whose we were,
and who we were accountable to.
We knew we were loved and valued.
And for that, I am forever thankful!
I hope we have made you proud!

ACKNOWLEDGEMENTS

First, I give glory and honor to Jesus Christ, my Lord and Savior, who planted a desire in my heart to nurture girls. That desire grew into a program/curriculum that can reach beyond my limited scope.

I want to thank the people who walked with me on this journey – from idea, to program development, to program implementation, to the copyright and trademark, to the publishing of this book.

Lamisha Hines – a friend and colleague who sought me out to conduct my G.I.R.L.S. Program with her Rhosebuds girls' group of the Theta Upsilon Sigma Chapter Alumnae Chapter of Sigma Gamma Rho Sorority in 2018. She was so enthusiastic about the program that she wanted me to share it with her national sorority, Sigma Gamma Rho. This propelled me to officially publish the curriculum.

Dr. Ayana Martin – my baby girl who insisted that I copyright and publish my work because of all the time and energy I invested in perfecting the lessons.

Marina Banks, esq – my attorney and family friend who stepped in to guide me through the entire trademark/copyrighting process. It was truly above my pay grade and without her, this book simply would not have been published.

Debra "Sunny" Jefferson – my "best friend" cousin – who was not only my encourager and cheerleader, but also my manuscript reader, corrector, and editor.

Nashira Williams who created the AMAZING G.I.R.L.S. logo. You can see more of her artwork at https://bravesoulco.org. She can be contacted at bravesoulandco@gmail.com.

Brandon Hall – who took my pages and got the book published.

It takes a village and I am deeply grateful for my village.

TABLE OF CONTENTS

PREFACE:
THE GENESIS OF G.I.R.L.S.

The idea of this program is rooted in one, the wisdom of my mother and, two, in my baby girl's group of childhood friends.

1. When I was a teenager (*back in the year 1* 😬😫), I would cry to my mom that "they" were gossiping about me. My mother's response was always the same: "You must really be something because they are always thinking about you. Because, in order for them to be talking about you, you have to be on their mind." Then she'd ask me, "How often do you think about them?" And my answer was always the same, "not until I'm told what they were saying about me." Then she'd sigh and say, "That is so sad; here they are, so consumed with you, and they don't even cross your mind." Then she'd just shake her head.

   Wisdom learned from my Mama:
   a) What others think of you is none of your business, especially if they do not know you (can you say social media commenters????).
   b) If you are busy doing what you enjoy, then you don't have time to be bothered about what others are saying about you.

2. The life success of my baby girl's group of childhood friends demonstrated how to successfully navigate adolescence. This group of kids were the "smart kids" in middle school. They were the first middle school class in Pasadena Unified School District that advanced to Geometry in 8th grade. They were envied, popular, and not bullied! What??? Smart kids not bullied??? How did that ***not*** happen???

   In retrospect, there was probably some bullying. However, this group did not notice because they were ***busy doing*** the activities that they enjoyed and social media was not a thing yet. If you are busy doing you, you don't have time to be concerned about everyone else.

Wisdom observed: Ain't nobody got time for that (hater-ism) if you are pursuing the interests that bring you joy and purpose to your life.

INTRODUCTION

The year is 2022 and my, my, how things have changed!!! The sense of community of yesteryear has transformed into the sense of me and mine. Sacrifice, discipline, and delayed gratification have become dirty words because they get in the way of what I want right now. The focus is on me, myself, and I, not on we, ourselves, and us.

"You do you, boo." "Live your life." "You only live once." "This is how I do it."

One of the consequences of this change is that the standards of society continuously shift – for this reason or for that cause. While change will happen as long as there is life, there must be a consistent standard from which to measure and guide. The problem with shifting standards is this: If standards are not consistent and reliable, then how can anything that is built, be able to stand – sturdy, secure, strong, and stable? For example, if my yardstick is 36 inches and your yardstick is 48 inches, and someone else's yardstick is 18 inches, how can anything be solidly built, let alone, last?

The same is true about standards in life. If the standards keep changing, how can a strong, sustainable, stable life be built to endure the challenges of life?

Below is a speech that was featured in both broadcast and print media in the mid 1960's by legendary ABC Radio news commentator and syndicated columnist, Paul Harvey, that predicted the issues prevalent today.

"If I Were the Devil"[1]
If I were the Prince of Darkness, I would want to engulf the whole earth in darkness.
I'd have a third of its real estate and four-fifths of its population, but I would not be happy until I had seized the ripest apple on the tree.

So, I should set about however necessary, to take over the United States.
I would begin with a campaign of whispers.
With the wisdom of a serpent, I would whisper to you as I whispered to Eve, "Do as you please."
To the young I would whisper "The Bible is a myth."
I would convince them that "man created God," instead of the other way around.
I would confide that "what is bad is good and what is good is square."
In the ears of the young married I would whisper that work is debasing, that cocktail parties are good for you. I would caution them not to be "extreme" in religion, in patriotism, in moral conduct.
And the old I would teach to pray — to say after me — "Our father which are in Washington."

Then I'd get organized.
I'd educate authors in how to make lurid literature exciting so that anything else would appear dull, uninteresting. I'd threaten TV with dirtier movies, and vice-versa.
I'd infiltrate unions and urge more loafing, less work. Idle hands usually work for me.
I'd peddle narcotics to whom I could, I'd sell alcohol to ladies and gentlemen of distinction,
I'd tranquilize the rest with pills.

---

[1] https://www.snopes.com/fact-check/if-i-were-the-devil/

If I were the Devil, I would encourage schools to refine young intellects, but neglect to discipline emotions; let those run wild. I'd designate an atheist to front for me before the highest courts and I'd get preachers to say, "She's right."

With flattery and promises of power I would get the courts to vote against God and in favor of pornography. Thus, I would evict God from the courthouse, then from the schoolhouse, then from the Houses of Congress. Then in his own churches I'd substitute psychology for religion and deify science.

If I were Satan, I'd make the symbol of Easter an egg

And the symbol of Christmas a bottle.

If I were the Devil, I'd take from those who have and give to those who wanted until I had killed the incentive of the ambitious. Then my police state would force everybody back to work. Then I would separate families, putting children in uniform, women in coal mines and objectors in slave-labor camps.

If I were Satan, I'd just keep doing what I'm doing and the whole world go to hell as sure as the Devil." It is very difficult to deny the truth of what Paul Harvey predicted.

G.I.R.L.S. (Girls Initiating Real Living Standards) Change Your View, Change Your World! provides a solution to this dilemma. This program was developed to equip girls of all ages (including young and seasoned women) to discover and develop who they are and whose they are, by giving them the tools to establish their own real living standards.

Completing these lessons will absolutely, positively shift your life in the best way possible.
You will
-   like yourself more,
-   appreciate yourself more,
-   value yourself more,
-   love yourself more, and
-   cherish who you are!!

When you cherish yourself, you will do those things that add to your life and avoid those things that subtract from your life. When you change your view, you change your world.
Failures can be viewed as stepping stones to success because you learn what doesn't work.
Every cloud has a silver lining. What the enemy means for evil, will work out for your good.

This is such an exceptional time for girls because there are many excellent girl empowerment programs available. However, what separates this program from other girls' empowerment programs is that it prepares the foundation/soil (mind), to receive the seed (real living standard) so it can get rooted, grow, flourish, and bear fruit (life success). If the foundation is weak, there will be little growth.

Just as a strong foundation is the key to a strong, stable, durable structure; a strong foundation of knowing who you are and whose you are is the key to grow through life – childhood, adolescence, and adulthood – successfully. *The wise man builds his house on a rock so that when storms come, it is not demolished but still stands.* So, let's check out the program!!!!

PROGRAM PURPOSE
To prepare and nurture the soil (young minds) to receive the seeds (real living standard) in order to yield a maximum life of success (bear fruit and more fruit).

PROGRAM TARGET
This program is designed for girls, elementary through high school.
Young and seasoned women benefit from the program content as well.

PROGRAM CURRICULUM
The **G.I.R.L.S.** curriculum is
- A strategic, layered, common sense, standards-based curriculum,
- That builds upon each concept presented in the previous lesson,
- In order to build a solid foundation upon which to develop a real living standard.

The curriculum is consistent with other researched based girl empowerment data.

The order of the lessons is critical because each concept builds upon the preceding one, so that participants will develop a solid sense of who they are, whose they are, and what their standards are. It is essential that the activities reinforce the Lesson of the Session. *The activities included in this curriculum are samples and are in no way exhaustive. There are many activities available – in workbooks, on the internet, on inspirational sites, etc. that can be used to instill the lessons.*

Each lesson concludes with a blank Lesson Page and inspiration cards that exemplify the lesson of the session. The inspiration cards can be pasted onto the blank Lesson Page to become a visual board - one for each lesson of the session.

LESSON FORMAT
Each lesson is formatted in the same way:
1. **A FOUNDATIONAL TRUTH** – scripture reference
2. **LESSON OF THE SESSION** – interpretation of the foundational truths
3. **DEIRDRE-ISM** – phrases I say regularly (most from me, some from others)
4. **IMPORTANT NOTE** – the concept of the lesson and how it applies in real life
5. **SUMMARY OF ACTIVITIES** – how the activities relate to the lesson concept
6. **LESSON SUMMARY** – summarizes the purpose and outcomes of each lesson
7. **LESSON OUTLINE** – the way the session is to be conducted
8. **ICE BREAKER** – activity with instructions
9. **SAMPLE EXERCISES** – activities with instructions

PROGRAM OUTCOME
Participants will
- Gain an increased sense of self-value and worth.
- Understand the connection between how you feel about yourself and what you feed your mind (via your eye-gate & ear-gate).
- Develop real living standards for their lives enabling them to establish boundaries.
- Discover the power within to get through difficulties/hardships to achieve their dreams.
- Understand the importance of caring for your body and developing support systems.

CHAPTER 1

TURNING THE SOIL OVER AND ADDING ORGANICS TO ENRICH THE SOIL TO ENCOURAGE GROWTH

LESSON 1

LESSON OUTLINE

AND

SAMPLE ACTIVITIES

LESSON 1: VALUABLE ME

FOUNDATIONAL TRUTH:
You are fearfully and wonderfully made! Psalm 139:14

LESSON OF THE SESSION:
You are awesome! There is none like you. You are a masterpiece, exquisitely made.
You are somebody, 'cause God don't make no junk!
You are awesome, so always be you, boo!

DEIRDRE-ISM:
It is better to be respected than liked.

IMPORTANT NOTE:
After the physical and security needs necessary for human existence are met, feeling loved is the next requirement in order to value one's self. Self-value is foundational to true self-esteem and self-actualization per Maslow's hierarchy of needs.

Value or self-worth is the one thing that we cannot instill into ourselves. That is because the origin of value comes from outside of ourselves. Others must pour into us in order for us to feel important. People invest time, energy and effort into things that are important to them. Parents who invest their time, energy, and effort in their children show it by their actions. Their actions show that their children have value because the parents make the time to show up and do things with them.

Children need their parents' presence so much more than their presents. When children get presents instead of presence, they are shown they are not worth the time, energy, and effort of their parents. They learn to seek presents to feel good about themselves. To continue to feel worthy or valuable, they will seek more and more presents to mask the feeling of not being valuable. This ultimately leaves them with feelings of emptiness and unworthiness.

I am certain you know someone who chases things in order to feel good about themselves. When you know that you have value, you realize that it is better to be respected than liked.

ACTIVITIES FOR VALUABLE ME:
The activities examine the things that make you special and stand out from others; what makes you valuable, uniquely you – your strengths, personality, interests, likes, dislikes. etc. The lesson closes with the Valuable Me inspiration cards and poster.

LESSON SUMMARY:
You will look at yourself from a positive point of view – what is special about you, what do you like about yourself? You will learn to focus on your positives, your uniqueness, and your special talents. You will learn to reframe what you consider to be a negative into a positive, and conclude the lesson with the Valuable Me inspiration cards and poster.

LESSON 1   VALUABLE ME

ICE BREAKER: THE NAME GAME

A fun introduction activity that has a positive twist to it. The game introduces each participant and helps everyone to remember each other's name. The positive twist is that each participant has to find a positive adjective that begins with the same letter of their name to precede their name. The first participant would say "Hi! My name is Amazing Anna." The next participant would say "She is Amazing Anna and I am Dynamic Demetria". The game continues until every participant has been introduced. Self-value gets watered in the participants as they call each other by their positive names throughout the entire program, thereby planting the positive attribute into their psyche.

ELEMENTARY
LESSON 1

VALUABLE ME
I am awesome!
You are fearfully & wonderfully made!   Psalms 139:14

Introduction to G.I.R.L.S.
Ice breaker: The Name Game

Lesson of the Session: You are awesome! There is no one like you!
Know who you are & whose you are.
You are somebody, because God don't make no junk!
If you know this, you know you have value.

Deirdre-ism: It is better to be respected than liked.

Activities:
  1. All About Me Worksheet
  2. My Favorite Things Worksheet
  3. Valuing Me, Myself & I Worksheet
  4. Inspiration Cards

Lesson of the session:
_____
_____

Something I learned:
_____
_____

Other things I thought about:
_____
_____

ALL ABOUT ME WORKSHEET

1. My full name is _____ _____ _____
                           (first)   (middle)   (last)

2. I have a nickname   ____ Yes   ____No   My nickname is _____.

3. I live in _____.
                (city)

4. I live with _____.

5. There are _____ people in my family.

6. I am the ____ oldest ____ youngest ____ in the middle.

7. In my home, I have to do _____.

8. One thing I do well is _____.

9. I am ____ handed   ____ handed

10. My hair is

  ___ long   ___ kinky   ___ straight
  ___ short   ___ curly   ___ thick
  ___ shoulder length   ___ wavey   ___ thin

11. My eyes are   ___dark brown   ___light brown   ___green   ___blue   ___hazel
___blue grey

12. I   ___ do   ___ do not   wear glasses.

MY FAVORITE THINGS

1. Color/colors _____.

2. Animal/animals _____.

3. Place to go _____.

4. Song _____.

5. TV show _____.

6. Movie _____.

7. Food _____.

8. Clothes _____.

9. Book _____.

10. Instrument _____.

VALUING ME, MYSELF & I

I like what I see when I look at me:
(What do I like about me?)

_____
_____
_____
_____

Who influences me?

_____
_____
_____
_____

Things I like:

_____
_____
_____
_____

Who do I listen to?

_____
_____
_____
_____

Things that make me happy:

_____
_____
_____
_____

Who do I answer to?

_____
_____
_____
_____

Things I like to do:

_____
_____
_____
_____

SECONDARY
LESSON 1

VALUABLE ME
I am awesome!
You are fearfully & wonderfully made!   Psalms 139:14

Introduction to G.I.R.L.S.
Ice breaker: The Name Game

Lesson of the Session: You are awesome! There is no one like you!
Know who you are & whose you are.
You are somebody, because God don't make no junk!
If you know this, you know you have value.

Deirdre-ism: It is better to be respected than liked.

Activities:
1. You Are Priceless! [2]
2. All About Me Activity
3. Our Greatest Fear [3]
4. Life's ABCs
5. Inspiration Cards

Lesson of the session:

_____

_____

Something I learned:

_____

_____

Other things I thought about:

_____

_____

2 Ralph Andrus, 2007, May 24, $20 Bill Faith Sermon; https://sermons.faithlife.com/sermons/18616-the-dollar20-dollar-bill
3 Marianne Williamson

ACTIVITY: YOU ARE PRICELESS!

A story that exemplifies how people retain their value even when they have been bruised, beaten and trampled upon.

PRICELESS

A well-known speaker started off his seminar
by holding up a $20 bill. In the room of 300,
he asked, "Who would like this $20 bill?"

Hands started going up. He said, I am going to give this $20 to one of you
But first, let me do this. He proceeded to crumple the dollar bill up.
He then asked, "Who still wants it?"
Still the hands were up in the air.

Well, he replied, what if I do this? And he dropped it on the ground
and started to grind it into the floor with his shoe.
He picked it up, now all crumpled and dirty.
"Now who still wants it?"
Still the hands went into the air.
I hope you have all learned a very valuable lesson.
No matter what I did to the money, you still wanted it
because it did not decrease in value.
It was still worth $20.

Many times in our lives, we are dropped,
crumpled, and ground into the dirt by the
decisions we make and the circumstances that
come our way. We feel as though we are worthless.
But no matter what has happened or what will happen,
you will never lose your value.

Dirty or clean, crumpled or finely creased,
You are still priceless!!

Always remember that!

ACTIVITY: ALL ABOUT ME INVENTORY
A survey about participants interests, thoughts, and expectations from the program.

CHANGE YOUR VIEW, CHANGE YOUR WORLD
Planting empowerment seeds to grow a life of success!

All About Me Inventory

This section is to be filled out by the participant.
Answer honestly and the best that you can.

_____

Name

Planting empowerment seeds to grow a life of success.

THIS PROGRAM WAS DESIGNED JUST FOR YOU!
You are encouraged to share and participate fully in the program.
What is said in the group, stays in the group.
We look forward to spending time with you and having FUN!

Name _____   Date _____

1. How did you come to be in the program?
_____
_____
_____

2. What expectations do you have?
_____
_____
_____

3. List 3 things you like about yourself. Explain why.
    1. _____
       _____
    2. _____
       _____
    3. _____
       _____

4. List 3 things you want to change about yourself. Explain why.
    1. _____
       _____
    2. _____
       _____
    3. _____
       _____

5. Do you like school? Explain why or why not. _____
_____
_____
_____

6. What is your favorite gift to give? Why? _____
_____
_____
_____

Name _____   Date _____

7. What is your favorite gift to receive? Why? _____
_____
_____

8. If you could have anything in the world, what would it be? _____
_____
_____

9. A Little More About Me...
   - Type of music I like to listen to _____
   - Type of book I like to read _____
   - My favorite song _____
   - My favorite TV show _____
   - My favorite sport _____
   - My favorite movie _____
   - My favorite color _____
   - My favorite hobby _____
   - What I like best about school _____

10. Why do you want to spend the next 9 weeks I the G.I.R.L.S. program?
_____
_____
_____
_____
_____

OUR GREATEST FEAR

"it is our light not our darkness that most frightens us"

Our deepest fear is not that we are inadequate.
Our deepest fear is that we are powerful beyond measure.
It is our light not our darkness that most frightens us.
We ask ourselves, who am I to be brilliant, gorgeous,
talented and fabulous?

Actually, who are you not to be?
You are a child of God.
Your playing small does not serve the world.
There's nothing enlightened about shrinking so that other
people won't feel insecure around you.

We were born to make manifest the glory of
God that is within us.

It's not just in some of us; it's in everyone.
And as we let our own light shine,
we unconsciously give other people
permission to do the same.

As we are liberated from our own fear,
Our presence automatically liberates others.

—Marianne Williamson

LIFE'S ABC'S

Avoid negative people, places and things.

Believe in yourself.

Consider things from every angle.

Don't give up and don't give in.

Enjoy life today. Yesterday is gone. Tomorrow may never come.

Family and friends are hidden treasures; seek them and enjoy their riches.

Give more than you planned.

Hang onto your dreams.

Ignore those who try to discourage you.

Just do it.

Keep trying, no matter how hard it seems. It will get easier.

Love yourself also.

Make dreams happen.

Never lie, cheat or steal. Always strike a fair deal.

Open your eyes and see things as they really are.

Practice makes perfect.

Quitters never win and winners never quit.

Read and learn about everything important to you.

Stop procrastinating.

Take control of your own destiny.

Understand yourself in order to better understand others.

Visualize your dreams.

Want your dream more than anything.

X-celerate your efforts.

You are a unique individual. Nothing can replace you.

Zero in on your goals and GO FOR THEM!

LESSON 1

VALUABLE ME
I am awesome!
You are fearfully & wonderfully made! Psalms 139:14

Your mission: feel good about who you are. what you do. how you think. and how you look- without needing anybody's approval!
karen Salmansohn
© notsalmon.com

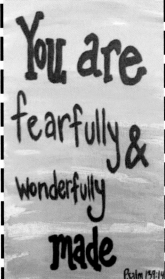

You are fearfully & wonderfully made
Psalm 139:14

VALUING YOURSELF

Important

"LOVE YOURSELF GIRL OR NOBODY WILL. NO NEED TO FIX WHAT GOD ALREADY PUT HIS PAINTBRUSH ON."

you're as amazing as you let yourself be...

I Know I'm SOMEBODY 'cause God Don't Make No JUNK

You are AMAZING.
You are IMPORTANT.
You are SPECIAL.
You are UNIQUE.
You are KIND.
You are PRECIOUS.
You are LOVED.

always remember you're BRAVER THAN YOU BELIEVE STRONGER THAN YOU SEEM smarter than you think ★★★ & TWICE AS BEAUTIFUL AS ★★★ you'd ever imagine

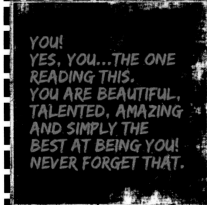

YOU! YES, YOU...THE ONE READING THIS. YOU ARE BEAUTIFUL, TALENTED, AMAZING AND SIMPLY THE BEST AT BEING YOU! NEVER FORGET THAT.

CHAPTER 2

BUILD A ROBUST INSECT ECOLOGY FOR BIOLOGICAL CONTROL OF PESTS

LESSON 2

LESSON OUTLINE

AND

SAMPLE ACTIVITIES

LESSON 2: KNOW THYSELF

FOUNDATIONAL TRUTH:
For as she thinks, so she is.   Proverbs 23:7

LESSON OF THE SESSION:
Knowing who you are and whose you are will keep you on the right path.
Who am I, who am I accountable to, who do I answer to?
I know I'm somebody because God don't make no junk!

DEIRDRE-ISM:
Never make yourself uncomfortable to make someone else comfortable.

IMPORTANT NOTE:
Once you understand and know that you have value, then you need to discover yourself –
- What do you like?
- What do you not like?
- Do you like being around a lot of people of just a few?
- What is interesting to you?
- What do you do well?
- What bothers you, what irritates you?
- What makes you really angry; etc.

When you get to know yourself, you become comfortable with yourself. When you become comfortable with yourself, you learn to like yourself. And it is very important that you like yourself because everywhere you go, there you are. You cannot hide from yourself.

When you know and like yourself, then you can make the choices that are right for you. When you make the choices that are right for you, you will do those things that are interesting to you. Pursuing what is interesting to you puts you in the position to explore, learn, and grow in those areas. Growing into your self will put you in the

position where you will not make yourself uncomfortable in order to make someone else comfortable.

ACTIVITIES FOR KNOW THYSELF:
The activities will delve further into becoming well acquainted with who you are, what your strengths are, and what you like. Knowing who you are strengthens your sense of self and gives you the security to try the things that you are interested in, even if no one else you know is interested in them. It enables you to like yourself and be yourself, which is so important because you take yourself with you wherever you go. You cannot hide from you, boo.

LESSON SUMMARY:
You will take an inward look at the things that make you, you. You'll explore your character traits, assess your strengths (areas that you are good) and weaknesses (areas that you can improve), look at the common denominators of successful teens and conclude the lesson with the Know Thyself inspiration cards and poster.

LESSON 2   KNOW THYSELF

ICE BREAKER: TOILET PAPER GAME

This is a fun way of sharing things (traits/characteristics/interests) about yourself.

A get-to-know-you activity that has the participants guessing what is up.

Hand the toilet paper roll to each participant and tell them to take as much as they think they will need and keep it. If they ask, "What's it for?" just say, "Take as much as you think you will need."

Don't give any guidance as to how much toilet paper they should unroll.

Once all of your participants have a wad of toilet paper, announce how the game works: each person must go around the room and share facts about themselves, one fact per square of toilet paper they unrolled.

ELEMENTARY
LESSON 2

KNOW THYSELF
Knowing who I am and whose I am.
For as she thinks, so she is. Proverbs 23:7

Ice Breaker: Name Game

Reflection: Last week I realized that I like …

Lesson of the Session:
Your income determines your outcome; what I think is what I become.
Knowing who you are and whose you are will keep you on the right path.
What I think really matters!

Deirdre-ism: Never make yourself uncomfortable to make someone else comfortable.

Activities:
1. Self-Acceptance & Self-Love:
    ▶ **YouTube Read Aloud**
    ➢ **I Like Myself** by Karen Beaumont
    ➢ **Same Different** by Calida Rawles
    ➢ **Big Hair, Don't Care** by Crystal Swain-Bates
    ➢ **I Love My Hair** – Sesame Street song
2. Knowing Myself – Loving Myself Worksheet
3. Mostly Like Me Worksheet
4. Inspiration Cards

Lesson of the session:
_____
_____

Something I learned:
_____
_____

Other things I thought about:
_____
_____

KNOWING MYSELF – LOVING MYSELF

"You are Smart. You are Good. You are Kind."*

1. 3 things I like about myself:
   - _____
   - _____
   - _____

2. 3 things I do well:
   - _____
   - _____
   - _____

shutterstock · 107466845

3. Who influences me? Who do I listen to? Who do I answer to?
   - _____
   - _____
   - _____
   - _____
   - _____

"YOUR *circle of influence dictates your path.*"

4. What do you tell yourself when things do not go the way you want?
   - _____
   - _____
   - _____
   - _____
   - _____

You are
AMAZING.
You are
IMPORTANT.
You are
SPECIAL.
You are
UNIQUE.
You are
KIND.
You are
PRECIOUS.
You are
LOVED.

MOSTLY LIKE ME

Check all the words that describe how you are usually.

___ Honest	___ Deceitful	___ Friendly	___ Shy
___ Patient	___ Impatient	___ Relaxed	___ Anxious
___ Happy	___ Moody	___ Helpful	___ Lazy
___ Joker	___ Serious	___ Respectful	___ Disrespectful
___ Listener	___ Talker	___ Determined	___ Give up easily
___ Leader	___ Follower	___ Loud	___ Quiet
___ Social	___ Loner	___ Careful	___ Careless
___ Polite	___ Rude	___ Responsible	___ Blamer
___ Leader	___ Follower	___ Sincere	___ Fake
___ Selfish	___ Generous	___ Kind	___ Mean
___ Giver	___ Taker	___ Fair	___ Biased

SECONDARY
LESSON 2

KNOW THYSELF
Knowing who I am and whose I am.
For as she thinks, so she is. Proverbs 23:7

Ice Breaker: Toilet Paper

Reflection: This week I realized that I was priceless when ….

Lesson of the Session: Knowing who you are and whose you are will keep you on the right path.

Deirdre-ism: Never make yourself uncomfortable to make someone else comfortable.

Activities:
1. My Character – What Do I Do & What Do I Stand for?
2. Asset Inventory[4]
3. Habits For Success
4. I Like What I See When I look At Me
5. Inspiration Cards

Lesson of the session:

_____
_____

Something I learned:

_____
_____

Other things I thought about:

_____
_____

[4] The Search Institute; https://searchinstitute.org/

MY CHARACTER:
(Character: What you do when no one is looking)

WHAT DO I DO? WHAT DO I STAND FOR?

Below are character trait statements. Identify those traits that describe you.
Put a "U" for usually, an "S" for sometimes, and an "N" for Never.

_____ I know what I need to do and I do it when it needs to be done. I am responsible.

_____ I forget to keep my promises.

_____ I am persistent. I don't give up easily.

_____ I don't always stand up for others.

_____ I am truthful in action and words.

_____ I am not concerned about others, especially when things don't go my way.

_____ I try to find something hopeful and positive about things. I am optimistic.

_____ When things are hard, I give up easily.

_____ I do the right thing, even if nobody's watching. I have integrity.

_____ When I am wrong, I will not admit it.

_____ I am reliable and loyal. I am trustworthy.

_____ I seldom express gratitude.

_____ I am courageous. I do the right thing even when it's difficult.

_____ I a really good at holding a grudge.

_____ I will stand up for others. I am fair minded.

_____ I will cheat if I believe I can get away with it.

_____ I am thankful and show others my gratitude.

_____ I am not always truthful, especially if I'm in trouble.

_____ I lend a helping hand to others and seldom hold a grudge.

_____ I like being a rebel, breaking the rules.

_____ I easily forgive people who hurt me.

_____ I easily get an attitude.

_____ I work together to help others.

_____ I try to do the least possible.

_____ I put forth my best effort.

_____ If I don't know you or like you, I will ignore you.

_____ I treat others the way I want to be treated. I respect others.

_____ It's hard for me to listen when I am mad.

_____ I follow the rules.

Character is demonstrated by behavior.

Areas I do well: Areas I need to improve:

_____   _____

_____   _____

_____   _____

40 Developmental Assets Checklist

What Do I Have Going for Me? Check all boxes that apply.

SUPPORT

❏ 1. I receive high levels of love and support from family members.

❏ 2. I can go to my parent(s) or guardian(s) for advice and support and have frequent in-dept conversations with them.

❏ 3. I know some non-parent adults I can go to for advice and support.

❏ 4. My neighbors encourage and support me.

❏ 5. My school provides a caring, encouraging environment.

❏ 6. My parent(s) or guardian(s) help me succeed in school.

EMPOWERMENT

❏ 7. I feel valued by adults in my community.

❏ 8. I am given useful roles in my community.

❏ 9. I serve in the community one hour or more each week.

❏ 10. I feel safe at home, in school and in the community.

BOUNDARIES & EXPECTATIONS

❏ 11. My family sets standards for appropriate behavior and monitors my whereabouts.

❏ 12. My school has clear rules and consequences for behavior.

❏ 13. Neighbors take responsibility for monitoring my conduct.

❏ 14. Parent(s) and other adults model positive, responsible behavior.

❏ 15. My best friends' model responsible behavior.

❏ 16. My parent(s)/guardian(s) and teachers encourage me to do well.

CONSTRUCTIVE USE OF TIME

❏ 17. I spend three hours or more each week in lessons or practice in music, theater or other arts.

❏ 18. I spend three hours or more each week in school or community sports, clubs or organizations.

❏ 19. I spend one hour or more each week in religious services or participating in spiritual activities.

❏ 20. I go out with friends "with nothing special to do" 2 or fewer nights each week.

COMMITMENT TO LEARNING

❏ 21. I want to do well in school.

❏ 22. I am actively engaged in learning.

❏ 23. I do an hour or more of homework each school day.

❏ 24. I care about my school.

❏ 25. I read for pleasure 3 or more hours each week.

POSITIVE VALUES

❏ 26. I believe it is very important to help other people.

❏ 27. I want to help promote equality and reduce world poverty and hunger.

❏ 28. I can stand up for what I believe.

❏ 29. I tell the truth even when it's not easy.

❏ 30. I can accept and take personal responsibility.

❏ 31. I believe it is important not to be sexually active or to use alcohol or other drugs.

SOCIAL COMPETENCE

❏ 32. I am good at planning ahead and making decisions.

❏ 33. I am good at making and keeping friends.

❏ 34. I know and am comfortable with people of different cultural/racial/ethnic backgrounds.

❏ 35. I can resist negative peer pressure and dangerous situations.

❏ 36. I try to resolve conflict nonviolently.

POSITIVE IDENTITY

❏ 37. I believe I have control over many things that happen to me.

❏ 38. I feel good about myself.

❏ 39. I believe my life has a purpose.

❏ 40. I am optimistic about my future.

HABITS TO DEVELOP IN ORDER TO ACHIEVE SUCCEESS

1. Be responsible for you and your actions. Accept your responsibility.
2. Be proactive. Anticipate what could happen and come up with possible solutions.
3. Begin with the goal you want to achieve. Anticipate and plan each action step to get there. For example – if you want to get an A on the Periodic Table of Elements. First get a Table and then develop a strategy to learn them, starting with the ones you are familiar with. Then develop a system to learn the others, testing yourself regularly until you have learned them all.
4. Get your priorities straight. Do the important things first.
5. Seek buy in from everyone you are working with. If people have a vested interest in something, then they will fully cooperate.
6. Listen to people rather than hearing them. When people feel like they are listened to, they are more cooperative.
7. Work smarter, not harder. It accomplishes more with less waste.
8. Work together cooperatively. A team achieves more.
9. Continue learning. It keeps you updated and relevant. It makes things work better and smoother.

These habits will help you to

- Prioritize your life
- Prioritizing your life will help you control your life.
- Prioritizing your life will help you to be disciplined.
- More discipline will have you saying yes to those things that benefit you.
- More discipline will help you make better decisions.
- It will help you define your standards and what matters to you most.
- It will improve your relationships with people – parents, teachers, friends, etc.
- It will help you to work smarter not harder.
- It will increase your confidence.
- You will find your balance between school, friends and everything else.
- You will be more content and happier.

What are the steps you need to take to develop the habits of success?

1. _____
2. _____
3. _____
4. _____
5. _____
6. _____

I LIKE WHAT I SEE WHEN I LOOK AT ME

What do I like about me?

Things I do well:

Things that make me happy:

LESSON 2

KNOW THYSELF

Knowing who I am and whose I am.

For as she thinks, so she is. Proverbs 23:7

INSPIRATION CARDS: KNOW THYSELF

Never make yourself
uncomfortable
To make someone
else
comfortable

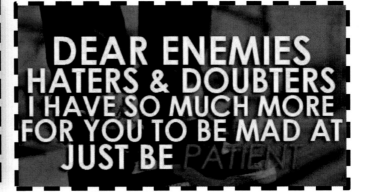
DEAR ENEMIES
HATERS & DOUBTERS
I HAVE SO MUCH MORE
FOR YOU TO BE MAD AT
JUST BE PATIENT

I know who I am,
I know what I believe,
and that's all I need
to know.

Proud to be me!!

www.multicultural-art.co.uk

I
AM
Important

SELF-LOVE

If you are not being treated with the love & respect you deserve, check your "PRICE TAG." Perhaps you've marked yourself down. It's "YOU" that determines what your worth by what you accept. Get off the "CLEARANCE RACK" and get behind the glass case where "Valuables" are kept. **Bottom line, "VALUE" yourself more**

Stop comparing yourself to others. You are you, nobody else could be you, even if they tried to be. You are unique and beautiful. Nobody else is you.

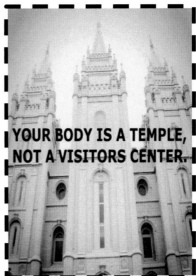
YOUR BODY IS A TEMPLE, NOT A VISITORS CENTER.

CHAPTER 3

GIVE UP THE CHEMICALS;
PESTICIDES KILL BOTH PEST AND BENEFICIAL INSECTS INDISCRIMINATELY.

LESSON 3

LESSON OUTLINE

AND

SAMPLE ACTIVITIES

LESSON 3: CHARACTER DEVELOPMENT – CHOICES

FOUNDATIONAL TRUTH:
Do not be misled: "Bad company corrupts good character." 1Corinthians 15:33

LESSON OF THE SESSION:
What I think is what I become.
What influences me? What am I watching?
What am I listening to? Who do I want to be like?

DEIRDRE-ISM:
Walk in integrity, so you can hold your head up
whether praised or persecuted

IMPORTANT NOTE:
Once we know our value/worth and discover our likes, strengths, reactions, and so on, then we are on the road to making choices that can be beneficial or detrimental to us. Many times, we work diligently to create the reputation we have, by the choices we consistently make. We become how we think and act.

- We talk constantly in class, then get upset when the teacher accuses us when talking is heard.
- We overexaggerate everything trying to impress, then get offended when we're called a liar.
- We must know as much as possible about everyone, then get upset when we're called a gossip.
- We must have designer everything, then get mad when we're called bougie.
- We make promises and forget to follow through, then get upset when we're called undependable.
- We want others to be there for us and forget to show up for others, then get mad when we're called flakey.

How you think and interact with people will determine how people will think and interact with you.

That's why it is so important to think before you act and consider the choices you make. What you think determines what you will do. What you do will determine what the outcome will be – whether you add positivity or negativity, whether you can be trusted or not, whether you can be depended upon or not. When you learn this, you will be able to walk in integrity and hold your head up whether you are praised or persecuted.

SUMMARY OF ACTIVITIES:
The activities will take inventory of who influences you in your life – home, school, community. You will reflect on your feelings about yourself, how you behave when no one is looking, and how you choose to react to challenges.

LESSON SUMMARY:
You will learn about character development and being responsible for your thoughts, words, and behavior. You will learn how the influences in your life impact you and your behavior. You will learn to identify what gets you going and how to control your response. You will learn how to get better at thinking for yourself and choosing the path that's best for you.

LESSON 3   CHARACTER DEVELOPMENT – CHOICES

ICE BREAKER: GOSSIP, GOSSIP

This is a fun activity that shows how important correct communication is and how easily what is said can be distorted. The activity begins by the facilitator whispering a sentence into the ear of the first participant, only once, with cupped hands so the others cannot hear. The recipient then whispers what she heard to the next participant, only once, with cupped hands so the others cannot hear. This continues with each participant until the last. The last participant repeats what she heard. It is hilariously amazing to see how much the original sentence has changed. It reinforces the need ensure the message received is the message sent.

LESSON 3

CHARACTER DEVELOPMENT: CHOICES
What I think is what I become.
Do not be misled: "Bad company corrupts good character." 1Corinthians 15:33

Icebreaker: Gossip, Gossip

Reflection: What makes me valuable?

Lesson of this Session:
You become what you think. What influences you?
What are you watching? What are you listening to? Who do you want to be like?

Deirdre-ism: Walk in integrity so you can hold your head up whether praised or persecuted.

Developing Character:
a) You become who you surround yourself with (birds of a feather flock together)
b) Your personal power – personal power versus role power
c) You are responsible for your words and behavior
d) You do have a choice
e) Identify what gets you going & learn to control your responses

Influences: family, friends, teachers, mentors, TV, movie stars, singers, song, lyrics, etc.
What are you feeding your mind? How does that influence your choices?

1. Define responsible (response – able; being able to respond) _____
2. Define choice _____
3. Do you take responsibility/accountability for your choices? How? _____
   _____

Activities:
1. Trent Shelton: Know Your Circle ▶ **YouTube** https://www.youtube.com/watch?v=iUYVVIC0wFs
2. Who Influences You Worksheet
3. Self-Value Survey
4. Understanding Power – Personal Power vs Role Power
5. You Got The Power - Being Responsible For Your Feelings, Words, And Behavior
6. Understanding Feelings
7. Inspiration Cards

Lesson of the session: _____

Something I learned: _____

Other things I thought about: _____

ACTIVITY: WHO'S INFLUENCING YOU?

Look at the influences in your life and how that reflects in your day-to-day life – how you feel, think, and act to the things in your life; how you are the boss of you and choose how to behave and respond.

Who Feeds You?

Important

- Family

- Friends

- School

- Church

ACTIVITY: SELF-VALUE SURVEY
How you see and feel about yourself.

SELF VALUE
"You Is Smart; You Is kind; You Is Important*."

1. List 3 things you like about yourself:
a. _____ b. _____ c. _____
2. List 3 things you want to change about yourself:
a. _____ b. _____ c. _____
3. Who controls you? _____
4. Who do you depend on? _____
5. Who do you answer to? _____

Check all that applies to you

☐ I stand up for what I believe in   ☐ I prefer to follow the crowd
☐ I feel good about who I am   ☐ I tend to feel less that my peers
☐ I am not concerned with being popular ☐ I worry about what others think of me

☐ I am confident   ☐ I act confident to hide my insecurities
☐ I face my problems head on   ☐ I avoid unpleasant things (ex. drugs)
☐ I complete the goals I set   ☐ Most things don't work out for me

How Do I Handle Challenges?

Thoughts leads to actions. Actions lead to consequences.
What I tell myself leads to what I do. What I do leads to what happens next.

What controls do I have to help me get through challenges?

1. Positive self-talk

_____
_____

2. What actions do I take? What do I do?

_____
_____

3. What happens when I do what I do? (consequences)

_____
_____

4. Who do I go to for help?

_____
_____

POWER

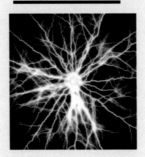

PERSONAL POWER   VS   ROLE POWER

Your skill,
your ability,
your knowledge,
to influence others

Built into roles or jobs
such as:
Parents, teachers,
police, babysitters,
coaches, etc.

I am responsible for
what I think,
what I say,
what I choose,
what I do.

YOU GOT THE POWER!!!

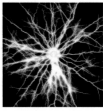

Even though you are just a kid, you do have power.
You are the boss of you. You are in control of what you do.
Name some things that you have power(control) over (ex., your thoughts, your words, your actions, etc.):
1. _____
2. _____
3. _____

Because you have power over what you think, say, and do, you can make choices about what you think, what you feel, and what you do.
Because you can make choices, you are responsible for your thoughts, feelings, actions, and behaviors.

You CAN choose what you think.
You CAN choose how you feel.
You CAN choose what you do.
You CAN choose how you react.
You CAN choose how you behave.

Knowing that you are able to choose, adds up to your personal power.

Power and choice scenarios:
What happens when you
- choose to study for spelling test or choose to play video games;
- choose to do your chores around the house (clean your room, put your toys up, take the trash out, etc.) or watch tv.

What are the consequences of each choice?
Not studying for your test _____
Studying for your test _____
Doing your chores around the house _____
Not doing your chores around the house _____
Watching TV instead of doing your chores _____
Who is responsible for each outcome? _____
Who has the power to choose a favorable outcome? _____

Name 3 other examples where you have the power to choose the better outcome:
1. _____
2. _____
3. _____

Remember that while you do have the power to choose, the choice you make does have outcomes.
So, think before you choose.

UNDERSTANDING FEELINGS

Feelings, simply put, is how you feel about something, someone, or a situation.
Feelings are not good, bad, right, or wrong. Feelings just are.
Bad things happen. Happy things happen. Sad things happen. Frustrating things happen.
Being able to describe your feelings is very important because there are many more words for feelings other than glad, bad, sad and mad. The more words you have to describe how you feel, the better you will be able to understand and express your feelings to others.

WORD BOX

Glad Happy Excited Joyful Cheerful Pleased Giddy Tickled Enthusiastic Satisfied

Sad Unhappy Sorrowful Downhearted Gloomy Dejected Depressed Heavyhearted

Mad Angry Furious Enraged Annoyed Irritated Infuriated Exasperated Temper

Bad Evil Inferior Rotten Naughty Disorderly Disgusting Unruly Lousy Intolerable

---

Choose words from the word box to describe how you might feel in each scenario.

Scenario #1:
Your parents went out and left you to watch your little sister. You know your sister loves opening up the kitchen cabinets and throwing all the contents on the floor. Your best friend texts you about the latest tick tock challenge and you get caught up in texting with your friend when you hear a loud crash from the kitchen. You rush in and find a mess and your little sister crying with a bump on her head.

1. What words describe how you feel? _____

2. Why do you feel the way you do? _____
_____

3. What would you do different? _____
_____

Scenario #2:
You have been trying to improve your school grades. You decided to spend more time on your studies and spend less time on social media. You missed activities with your friends and the latest social media trends. At the mid-term, you find out that you have improved in all your classes but one.

1. What words describe how you feel? _____

2. Why do you feel the way you do? _____
_____

3. What would you do different? _____
_____

The more you understand yourself and your feelings, the more power you will have over yourself.
The more power you have over yourself, the better choices you will make.
The better choices you make, the better the outcomes in your life.

CHARACTER DEVELOPMENT: CHOICES
What I think is what I become.

Do not be misled: Bad company corrupts good character. 1 Corinthians 15:33

IF YOU NEVER TRY YOU'LL NEVER KNOW

Change your thoughts

Transform your life.

YOUR *thoughts* ARE *colored* BY WHAT *you*...

The 3 C's in your life:

CHOICE, CHANCE, CHANGE.

You must make the choice, to take the chance, if you want anything in life to change.

you are today where your thoughts have brought you; you will be tomorrow where your thoughts take you.

People inspire you or they drain you. Pick them wisely.

Everything in your life is a reflection of a choice you have made. If you want a different result, make a different choice.

CHAPTER 4

USE COMPOST AND MULCHES; NATURAL AMENDMENTS THAT IMPROVE SOIL CONDITIONS.

LESSON 4

LESSON OUTLINE

AND

SAMPLE ACTIVITIES

LESSON 4: CHARACTER DEVELOPMENT: SELF DISCIPLINE

FOUNDATIONAL TRUTH:
A good name is better than precious ointment… Ecclesiastes 7:1

LESSON OF THE SESSION:
Your income determines your outcome.
What you let in is what will come out.
Who and what you surround yourself with matters.

DEIRDRE-ISM
An attitude of gratitude will take you further than your aptitude!

IMPORTANT NOTE:

In this life you will have troubles; how do you make it through? Overwhelming situations make us feel as if we have no control – what's the point of it all? That is why what you are thinking, what you are saying to yourself, and who is influencing you is so critical. Are you telling yourself that you can do it, keep trying or are you telling yourself to give up, it's too hard? Are your influencers pouring a "you-can-do-it" spirit or a "it's-too-hard-take-the-easy-way-out" spirit into your life? It is important to know what is driving the choices and actions you take. It makes a difference how we view things. Which would you choose:

1. Be really smart but think you can't do it?
OR
2. Be not so smart but think you can do it?

If you think you can't, you can't. If you think you can, you can. Knowledge and hard work are good things to have, but a good "can do" attitude will take you further.

Knowledge and hard work require discipline. Discipline says yes to the thorough and no to the short cuts. Discipline says yes to staying on track and no to distractions. Discipline sets priorities and completes what's most important. Discipline keeps you on the right road to your interests and goals. It keeps you

from unnecessary detours and dead ends. Discipline will let you know what to let in and what to let go so that you can achieve your goals. Now you can see why in this age of the instantaneous, discipline is seen as a dirty word. You will learn that an attitude of gratitude will take you further than your aptitude.

SUMMARY OF ACTIVITIES:

The activities will examine responsibility, accountability, and their relationship with self-discipline/self-control. The lessons will explore who is responsible for your attitude, behavior, and actions; how to establish real living standards in what you will do – where you will go, who you hang out with, etc.; and how to reinforce those real living standards which produce positive outcomes.

LESSON SUMMARY:

You will learn that you are responsible for your thoughts, your behavior, and your actions; so, think for yourself. Discipline will get you to establish priorities and boundaries that keep you on track. You will learn how to handle the challenges that life throws your way and revisit the habits of effective teens. The lesson concludes with the Self-Discipline Character Development inspiration cards and poster.

LESSON 4   CHARACTER DEVELOPMENT: SELF DISCIPLINE

ICE BREAKER: MIX & MEET

This activity is a fun way to learn more about the participants. Each person grabs a small handful of candies but be sure to tell them not to eat them yet. (Use colorful candies like M&Ms, Skittles, Smarties)

Each person takes a turn to share a fact about themselves for every piece of candy they have grabbed. Each color will have a topic assigned to it.

EXAMPLE:

Purple = Most memorable or embarrassing moment

Green = Favorite hobbies

Yellow = Favorite foods

Red = People you admire

Orange = Music & movies you like

The fact they share must be associated with the color of the candies they picked. For example, if they have three blue and one green, they would have to say three facts for the "blue topic" and one fact for the "green topic".

ELEMENTARY
LESSON 4

CHARACTER DEVELOPMENT – SELF DISCIPLINE
Your income determines your outcome.
A good name is better than precious ointment… Ecclesiastes 7:1

Icebreaker: Mix & Meet

Reflection: This week I am proud that I …….
         Review: Character Development – What I Think I Become

Lesson of the Session: What you let in, is what will come out.

Deirdre-ism:
An attitude of gratitude will take you further than aptitude, knowledge and hard work!

In this life you will have troubles; how do you make it through?
Over whelming situations make us feel as if we have no control – what's the point of it all?
I'm just a kid, what can I control?

Summary: the good and the bad
Who is the boss of you, who controls you? _____
Who do you depend on? _____
Who do you answer to? _____
Do you stand up for what you believe in or do you follow the crowd? _____
How do you make decisions? _____

<u>**YOU ARE RESPONSIBLE FOR YOU, YOUR BEHAVIOR, YOUR ACTION.**</u>
<u>**SO, THINK FOR YOURSELF!!**</u>

Activities: 1. It's My Choice
           2. Problem Solving Map
           3. Inspiration Cards

Lesson of the session:
_____
_____

Something I learned:
_____
_____

Other things I thought about:
_____
_____

It's My CHOICE!

I can decide to feel good about me.
There is none like me!

WHAT IS UNIQUE ABOUT ME?

Name _____

One thing I love to do _____

My favorite season _____

My favorite animal _____

When I am happy, I _____

My favorite subject _____

I think it's important to _____

_____

My 3 closest friends

1. _____

2. _____

3. _____

I can decide to play fair so that everyone has fun and no one is not left out.

List ways everyone can be included.

_____

_____

_____

I can decide how to feel when something makes me angry.

Fill in the blank bubbles with feelings you can choose.

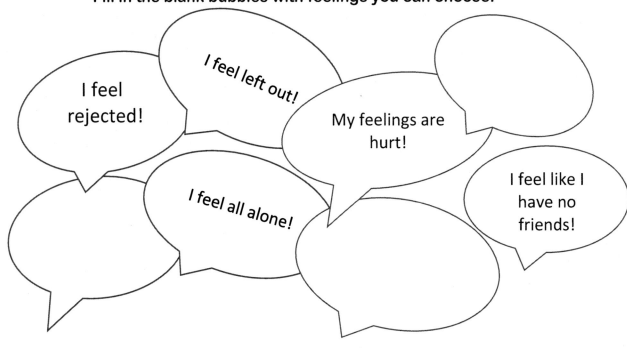

I feel rejected!

I feel left out!

My feelings are hurt!

I feel all alone!

I feel like I have no friends!

FILL IN THE BUBBLES WITH YOUR WORDS

I can decide to tell others how I feel
when they make me mad.

I can decide to solve my problems
without hurting others.

When I decide to make good choices, I feel better about myself.

I can choose to
include everyone
when I play.

I treat others the way
I want to be treated.

I can choose to
not hurt
others when I
disagree.

I can tell
others how I
feel when they
make me mad
without
hurting their
feelings.

I can choose how I
feel when something
makes me mad,

When I decide to make good choices, everyone is happier.

A PROBLEM-SOLVING STRATEGY

Everyone faces problems, kids as well as adults. It a part of this thing called life. When faced with a problem, what is needed is a way to resolve it in a positive way.

The worksheet below is a problem-solving tool to help you figure out a positive solution to a situation or problem that has come up in your life. Use it to think through the advantages and disadvantages of each possible solution to come up with the best one that ill work for you.

It uses the acronym **S-O-D-A-S** to implement each step.
Here is an example:
S – Situation: describe the situation
 A kid in school called me a bad name.
O – Options: what are the options/choices; make a list
 1. I could tell the teacher.
 2. I could hit the kid.
 3. I could ignore the kid and do something else.
D – Disadvantages – what are the disadvantages of each option
 1. I get labeled a tattle tale.
 2. I get suspended from school for hitting a kid.
 3. I could look like a wimp for doing nothing.
A – Advantages – what are the advantages of each option
 1. The teacher solves the problem & I don't get in trouble.
 2. I get my anger released and maybe the kid stops calling me names.
 3. The kid sees it doesn't bother me so he leaves me alone.
S – Solution – pick the solution that has the best advantages.
 Pick the solution that is best for you.
AND THEN IMPLEMENT THE SOLUTION – JUST DO IT!

Use the SODAS Problem Solving Map to solve a problem that you have had.

SODAS PROBLEM SOLVING MAP

S – Scenario – What is the situation?

O – Options – What are the choices?

1.	2.	3.

D – Disadvantages – What are they?

1.	2.	3.

A – Advantages – What are they?

1.	2.	3.

S – Solution – What is the best solution?

I

IMPLEMENT THE SOLUTION

SECONDARY
LESSON 4   **CHARACTER DEVELOPMENT:**
                 SELF-DICIPLINE/REAL LIVING STANDARDS
                   Your income determines your outcome!
              A good name is better than precious ointment… Ecclesiastes 7:1

Icebreaker: Mix & Meet

Reflection: This week I am proud that I …….

Lesson of the Session: What you let in, is what will come out.

Deirdre-ism:
An attitude of gratitude will take you further than your aptitude!

In this life you will have troubles; how do you make it through?
To your own self be true! Know who you are, whose you are and who you are accountable to.
Over whelming situations make us feel as if we have no control – what's the point of it all?
Knowing your boundaries will keep a safe perimeter around you, keeping out major danger.

The good and the bad
Who is the boss of you, who controls you? _____
Who do you depend on? _____
Who do you answer to? _____
Do you stand up for what you believe in or do you follow the crowd? _____
How do you make decisions? _____

You are responsible for you, your thoughts, and your actions; so, think for yourself.
Establish boundaries around yourself – what you will do and will not do, where you will go and will not go, who you will hang out with and not hang out with, etc.

Activities:
1. Self-Discipline/Setting Standards
2. Navigating the Troubles in Life
3. Coincidence or Not[5]
4. Review Habits of Success
5. Inspirational Cards

Lesson of the session:
_____
_____

Something I learned:
_____
_____

Other things I thought about:
_____
_____

5 https://www.projectmanagement.com/blog-post/18183/Attitude--Coincidence-or-Not--

SELF-DISCIPLINE AND STANDARDS

In this life there will be ups and downs, trials and challenges. When situations appear overwhelming and it seems easier to just give up rather than try, discipline and standards can help you to refocus, gain some control, and get things moving in the right direction. Discipline is the ability to achieve an outcome through controlling oneself. A standard is an established measurement, guide, rule, authority, or model.

From infancy through early childhood, caregivers took care of all your needs. They corrected (disciplined) you and that is how you learned what was right, what was wrong, and what was expected. This initial discipline came from outside of you – parent, caregivers, teachers, etc. As you grew older, you learned what was right, what was wrong, and what behavior was expected. So now, the discipline comes from within you.

Taking charge of your life means that you know what you should and should not do. When you are able to do what you are supposed to do, that strengthens your ability to control yourself. Self-discipline, self-restraint or self-control, is what can help you to get through unexpected situations. When you stop, think, and then act, instead of immediately reacting to the situation, you strengthen your self-discipline. Examples of self-restraint is you holding your tongue when someone offends you or you not hitting someone who shoves you.

Ways to increase your self-discipline, self-control and self-restraint:
1. Make the decision that you want to be more disciplined and controlled in your actions and responses. Write an example where you can be more controlled in your actions or responses.

_____

2. Do things that require more discipline and self-reliance like doing your own laundry.
    Write an example of what you can do to show more self-reliance.

_____

3. Learn the rules that determine what you can and cannot do. Set boundaries.
    Write an example of how you can set boundaries on what you should do and not do.

_____

4. Be accountable. Own your behavior. Do not blame others for your decisions and actions.
    Write an example of how you can be accountable for what you do.

_____

5. Do activities that require self-discipline like learning to play an instrument or volunteering.
    Write an example of an activity you would like to do that requires self-discipline.

_____

In this life you will have trouble. That is a sure thing. The thing is to learn how to successfully get through troubles without letting them get to you. Self-discipline, standards, and boundaries will help you navigate life's ups and downs.

When trouble comes a-calling:
1. What do your thoughts tell you? _____
   _____
2. Are these thoughts helpful or unhelpful? How so?
   Helpful _____
   Unhelpful _____
3. What happens after you think? What actions do you take? _____
   _____
4. What are the consequences of your actions? _____
   _____
5. When your actions become consistent, they become habits – things you automatically do. What actions of yours have become habits, ex., addressing adults as Mr. or Ms.? _____
   _____
6. Habits become your character – what you do when no one is looking, doing the right thing even if it's not popular, etc. What are some of your character traits? (ex. telling the truth)
   _____
7. Your character (how you are) becomes your destiny (how you will be). Name some of your character traits that will be a plus for you in the future. _____
   _____

Does what you usually do, help you successfully get through the situation?
     _____ Yes   Then continue doing what helps you gets through trouble in a positive way.
     _____ No   Then rethink what you can to do to gain some positive control.
- Rethink your thoughts – tell yourself you can get through this in a positive way.
- Tell yourself, I can do this, I will try, I will not give up, etc.
- Do the right thing because it is the right thing to do.
- Surround yourself with people who care about you and who can help in positive ways.

When the troubles of life get you down, think – what will help get me through them? Stop. Slow your roll. Think about what to do rather than react without thinking, so outcomes can be better. Tell yourself to do the right thing; that you can do it; that you will try; that you won't give up; and seek trustworthy people that support you.

COINCIDENCE OR NOT?

If....

ABCDEFGHIJKLM
NOPQRSTUVWXYZ

Equals...

1 2 3 4 5 6 7 8 9 10 11 12 13
14 15 16 17 18 19 20 21 22 23 24 25 26

Add up the letter values in the words below

K N O W L E D G E =

H A R D W O R K =

Both are important,
but fall short of 100%
BUT

A T T I T U D E =

SO

**COINCIDENCE
OR NOT?**

Your knowledge will let you
walk on the roads of success,
but oftentimes you will have to pass
The Hard Work Boulevard.
And when you reach the Hard Work
Boulevard and you feel lost
remember that your attitude will
always be your ultimate guide.

LESSON 4   **CHARACTER DEVELOPMENT:**
SELF-DICIPLINE/REAL LIVING STANDARDS
Your income determines your outcome!
A good name is better than precious ointment... Ecclesiastes 7:1

Everything in
your life
is a reflection
of a choice
you have made.
If you want
a different result,
make a different
choice.

When you can't control
what's happening,
challenge yourself to
control how you
respond to what's
happening. That's
where your power lies.

WRONG
is WRONG,
even if *everyone*
is doing it.

RIGHT
is RIGHT,
even if *no one*
is doing it.

"LOVE YOURSELF GIRL OR
NOBODY WILL. NO
NEED TO FIX WHAT GOD
ALREADY PUT HIS PAINTBRUSH ON."

NOPE.

I WILL NOT BE LAZY. I WILL NOT BE LIKE EVERYONE ELSE IN SOCIETY.
I WILL NOT ACCEPT WHAT I HAVE NOW IF I KNOW I DESERVE BETTER.
I WILL NOT SLEEP UNTIL I FINISH. I WILL NOT LEAVE UNTIL I'M DONE.
I WILL NOT TREMBLE INFRONT OF NEW CHALLENEGES. I WIL NOT
STOP UNTIL I STOP BREATHING. I WILL BE WHATEVER I WANT TO BE
EVEN IF IT TAKES SACRIFICE. EVEN IF I HAVE LITTLE TO GIVE. EVEN IF
IT TAKES TIME. EVEN IF I HAVE NO TIME AT ALL. I WILL SUCCEED.

Life is an echo.

What you send out – comes back.
What you sow – you reap.
What you give – you get.
What you see in others –
exists in you.
Do not judge - so you will
not be judged.
Radiate and give love
and love will come
back to you.

Let your light shine so
brightly that others can
see their way out of the dark.

I am thankful
for all those difficult people
in my life, they have shown
me exactly who I do not
want to be.

CHAPTER 5

SOW SEEDS IN PRE-MOISTEN THE MIX SO
THE SEEDS ARE NOT DISTURBED BY WATER AFTER PLANTING.

LESSON 5

LESSON OUTLINE

AND

SAMPLE ACTIVITIES

LESSON 5: HANDLING THE UPS & DOWNS OF LIFE

FOUNDATIONAL TRUTH:
I know the plans and thoughts I have for you...plans to give you a hope.
Jeremiah 29:11

LESSON OF THE SESSION:
You were born for such a time as this!
Believe in your destiny; You are here for a reason.
Life has bumps, troubles, & crashes – so what's the point?
To be a blessing; to be a help to others; to be a hope; to be an encouragement

DEIRDRE-ISM:
Treat others as you would like to be treated and make the world a better place.

IMPORTANT NOTE:
In this life, you will have trouble. What are you gonna do? How are you gonna handle the ups and downs in your life? Do you have hope, a positive outlook, and a strategy? The half-filled glass can be viewed as either half empty or half full. You know you are fearfully and wonderfully made. You know the plans for you are for a hope and a future. You know are here for a reason. You know you have a dream you want to achieve. You are here to achieve, to be a blessing, a help, and a hope to yourself and to others.

When you have hope, you will view trouble as a challenge – something to learn from, something to overcome. You will learn to change your response rather than try to change an unchangeable situation. That change in your view will change the outcome. Changing your responses by treating others as you want to be treated will make this world a better place.

SUMMARY OF ACTIVITIES:
The activities will explore the ups and downs in your life and how you have responded to those challenges. You will look at your future dreams, goals and interests. You will learn how to solve problems in a constructive way and learn how changing your view of a problem can change the outcome.

LESSON SUMMARY:
Believe in your destiny. You are a promise, a possibility. You were born for such a time as this. Learn the lessons life has for you. Master the life lesson, then you will be able to move on to the next one. Figure out how to solve problems in a positive way. Figure out how to change your reaction rather than change a situation you have no control over. Changing your reaction will change your outcome. The lesson concludes with the Handling the Ups & Downs of Life inspiration cards and poster.

LESSON 5   HANDLING THE UPS AND DOWNS OF LIFE

ICE BREAKER: SIT DOWN IF...

This activity is a way for everyone to participate without speaking and
yet share information about themselves. Get everyone to stand up.
Then read through the list below (you can use the list below or create one of your own).
When the last person sits, the activity is over.

- Sit down if you have eaten chocolate today
- Sit down if you are wearing purple
- Sit down if you were born in September
- Sit down if you have blue eyes
- Sit down if you are the youngest child
- you have broken a bone
- gone for two weeks without a shower
- can speak more than two languages
- You were born on the 31st day of any month.
- You have ever owned a pet rabbit or pet snake.
- You have broken more than 2 bones in your body.
- You regularly pick your nose when no one is looking.
- You have ridden in a limousine.
- You forgot your homework or lunch and your mom has brought it to you school this year.
- You're wearing a _____ shirt right now.
- You have seen a movie in the theatre in the past 10 days.
- You have ridden on a motorcycle.
- Your mom drives a mini-van.
- You've ever been to Disney World.
- You have green eyes.
- You've spent more than 30 hours playing video games in the past 10 days.
- You have never had stitches.
- You are good-looking but not conceited.
- Stand up if the person next to you just sat down and was wrong.
- Your cell phone has rung out loud while you were in class.
- You've made yourself vomit a rainbow on SnapChat this week.
- You've been on SnapChat since you got here tonight.
- You have never had a cavity.
- You have ridden on a camel.
- You have ridden in a limousine.
- You are currently grounded.
- Your mom drives a mini-van.
- You've been pulled by the cops in the past 6 months.

**ELEMENTARY
LESSON 5**

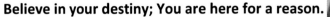

HANDLING THE UPS & DOWNS OF LIFE
Believe in your destiny; You are here for a reason.
I know the plans I have for you...plans to give you a hope and a future.   Jeremiah 29:11

Icebreaker: Sit Down If....

Reflection: This week _____ (something good) happened to me.

Review: Valuable Me; Know Yourself; Character Development

Lesson of the Session: You were born for such a time as this.
I am a promise; I am a possibility; I am a promise with a capital "P";
I am a great big bundle of potentiality
And I am learnin' to hear my voice; And I am tryin' to make the right choice;
I am a promise, to be anything I want to be.
Written by Bill and Gloria Gaither

Deirdre-ism: Treat others as you would like to be treated and make the world a better place.

Believe in your destiny; You are here for a reason
Life has bumps, troubles, & crashes – so what do you do?
Be a blessing; help to others; have hope; be encouraged.

What can be used to control your emotions when challenged?
1. Positive self-talk   3. Do something positive
2. Help others   4. Seek your support system

Activity: Handling the Ups & Downs of Life Worksheet
                Inspiration Cards

Lesson of the session:

_____

_____

Something I learned:

_____

_____

Other things I thought about:

_____

_____

HANDLING THE UPS AND DOWNS OF YOUR LIFE

How you feel has a huge impact on how you handle things. Feelings that make people feel good help you to have fun and enjoy life. Feelings that make people feel bad do not help you to have fun and enjoy life.

List feelings that make you feel good:

_____   _____   _____
_____   _____   _____
_____   _____   _____
_____   _____   _____

List some feelings that make you feel bad:

_____   _____   _____
_____   _____   _____
_____   _____   _____
_____   _____   _____

Learning to identify your feelings will help you to understand why you feel the way you do and will enable you to adjust your feelings in order to achieve a better outcome. Remember, it is ok to feel negative feelings such as anger, rejection, fear, etc. But when you feel this way, try not to hurt, mistreat, or damage others or property. Instead do these four things:

1. Ask yourself, what happened to make me feel the way I do?
2. Ask yourself, why am I feeling that the way I do?
3. Ask yourself, what choices do I have about the way I feel? Can I feel another way?
4. Decide on a way to handle the feeling in the most positive way.

Describe a situation that you did not handle in the best way possible: _____
_____
_____

Describe how you could have handled it in a better way using the 4 steps:
_____
_____
_____
_____

Everyone, no matter who they are, has ups and downs. The best way to handle them is to figure out what happened to make you feel the way you do, understand why you feel the way you do, then figure out the best way to respond to your feelings.

SECONDARY
LESSON 5

HANDLING THE UPS & DOWNS OF LIFE
Believe in your destiny; You are here for a reason.
I know the plans I have for you…plans to give you a hope and a future.   Jeremiah 29:11

Icebreaker: Sit Down If….

Reflection: This week _____ (something good) happened to me."

Lesson of the Session: You were born for such a time as this.
I am a promise; I am a possibility; I am a promise; with a capital P;
I am a great big bundle of potentiality
And I am learnin' to hear my voice; And I am tryin' to make the right choice;
I am a promise to be, anything I want to be.
Written by Bill and Gloria Gaither

Deirdre-ism: Treat others as you would like to be treated and make the world a better place.

Life has bumps, troubles, & crashes – so what's the point?
To be a blessing; to be a help to others; to be a hope; to be an encouragement

Activities:
1. My Life's Ups & Downs
2. Handling Your Ups & Downs
3. SODAs Method of Solving Problems
4. 90/10 Principle – It Will Change Your Life[6]
5. Inspiration Cards

Lesson of the session:

_____

_____

Something I learned:

_____

_____

Other things I thought about:

_____

_____

6 Stephen Covey – 90/10 Principle

ACTIVITY: MY LIFE'S UPS AND DOWNS

Make a timeline of your life, writing the age you were for each highlight and each low point in your life. Write things that have had an impact on you, regardless of how small.

My Life's Ups & Downs   Name: _____

GIRLS

Girls Initiating Real Living Standards

HANDLING THE UPS AND DOWNS OF YOUR LIFE
(Refer to the completed My Life's Ups & Downs timeline)

How you feel has a huge impact on how you handle things. Feelings that make people feel good help you to have fun and enjoy life. Feelings that make people feel bad do not help you to have fun and enjoy life.

List feelings that make you feel good:

_____   _____   _____
_____   _____   _____
_____   _____   _____
_____   _____   _____

List some feelings that make you feel bad:

_____   _____   _____
_____   _____   _____
_____   _____   _____
_____   _____   _____

Learning to identify your feelings will help you to understand why you feel the way you do and will enable you to adjust your feelings in order to achieve a better outcome. Remember, it is ok to feel negative feelings such as anger, rejection, fear, etc. But when you feel this way, try not to hurt, mistreat, or damage others or property. Instead do these four things:

1. Ask yourself, what happened to make me feel the way I do?
2. Ask yourself, why am I feeling that the way I do?
3. Ask yourself, what choices do I have about the way I feel? Can I feel another way?
4. Decide on a way to handle the feeling in the most positive way.

Describe a situation that you did not handle in the best way possible: _____
_____
_____

Describe how you could have handled it in a better way using the 4 steps:
_____
_____
_____
_____

Everyone, no matter who they are, has ups and downs. The best way to handle them is to figure out what happened to make you feel the way you do, understand why you feel the way you do, then figure out the best way to respond to your feelings.

A PROBLEM-SOLVING STRATEGY

Everyone faces problems, kids as well as adults. It a part of this thing called life. When faced with a problem, what is needed is a way to resolve it in a positive way.

The worksheet below is a problem-solving tool to help you figure out a positive solution to a situation or problem that has come up in your life. Use it to think through the advantages and disadvantages of each possible solution to come up with the best one that ill work for you.

It uses the acronym **S-O-D-A-S** to implement each step.
Here is an example:
S – Situation: describe the situation
     A kid in school called me a bad name.
O – Options: what are the options/choices; make a list
     1. I could tell the teacher.
     2. I could hit the kid.
     3. I could ignore the kid and do something else.
D – Disadvantages – what are the disadvantages of each option
     1. I get labeled a tattle tale.
     2. I get suspended from school for hitting a kid.
     3. I could look like a wimp for doing nothing.
A – Advantages – what are the advantages of each option
     1. The teacher solves the problem & I don't get in trouble.
     2. I get my anger released and maybe the kid stops calling me names.
     3. The kid sees it doesn't bother me so he leaves me alone.
S – Solution – pick the solution that has the best advantages.
     Pick the solution that is best for you.
AND THEN IMPLEMENT THE SOLUTION – JUST DO IT!

Use the SODAS Problem Solving Map to solve a problem that you have had.

SODAS PROBLEM SOLVING MAP

S – Scenario – What is the situation?

O – Options – What are the choices?

1.	2.	3.

D – Disadvantages – What are they?

1.	2.	3.

A – Advantages – What are they?

1.	2.	3.

S – Solution – What is the best solution?

IMPLEMENT THE SOLUTION

10/90 PRINCIPLE

Author Stephen Covey described a principle called the 10/90 principle. Ten percent of life is made up of what happens to you. Ninety percent of life is decided by how you react.
It will change your life (or at least the way you react to situations).

WHAT IS THIS PRINCIPLE?
10% of life is made up of what happens to you... 90% of life is decided by how you react.

WHAT DOES THAT MEAN?
We really have **NO** control over the 10% of what happens to us.
The 90% is different. **YOU** determine the 90%

HOW? By The Way You React.
You cannot predict how to control unplanned situation, such as an accident, a death, being late to school, in traffic, and so on. However, you can control your reaction. What you can do, is simple. Do not let circumstances, or people to fool you. YOU can control how you react!

Let's take this example:
You live with your father. He recently moved both of you into an apartment with a friend of his. As far as you knew, things were fine – you finally got situated in school, your father got a new job, and everything was going great. Out of the blue, your father's roommate, tells him that you guys have to move as soon as possible because her ex-boyfriend decided to come back, after dumping her and marrying someone else. ***What do you do now?***

Your father just started a new job so he doesn't have the money to find another apartment.
You just made new friends and your school is one bus ride away. Life looks unfair, doesn't it?
You feel like, your entire world is crumbling, all because of someone else's decision, which
YOU HAVE NO CONTROL over. ARE YOU WITH ME SO FAR?
Now, **THE WAY YOU REACT**, will determine **WHAT HAPPENS NEXT.**

Scenario A:
You curse and yell at your father for his stupid choices. He breaks down with guilt and shame. Next, you call your mother and yell at her for getting a divorce, and putting you in the middle of this mess. An argument follows. Now, you have a huge headache. You storm outside and hold your head with disbelief. You go back in and find your father beating himself up instead of getting ready for work. He rushes to dress for work and you rush to the bus to get to school. You miss your bus and your father has to drop you off at school. Because he has to take you to school, he drives 45 miles per hour in a 30-mph zone, gets pulled over by the police, and gets a speeding ticket. You finally arrive at school. You rush out of the car without saying goodbye to your father and arrive to your class 10 minutes late. Because you're late, you get assigned to detention. When asked to turn in your homework, you realize that you left your backpack at home. What a terrible day it is turning out to be. As the day continues, it seems to get worse and worse. You look forward to coming home. When you arrive home, you find a wedge in your relationship with your father.

WHY IS THERE A WEDGE IN THE RELATIONSHIP? Because of how you reacted in the morning.
WHY DID YOU HAVE A BAD DAY?

A) Did the roommate cause it?
B) Did your father cause it?
C) Did the policeman cause it?
D) Did you cause it?

The answer is: D

You had NO CONTROL over what happened with the roommate.
How you reacted in those 5 seconds is what caused your bad day!

Here is what could have happened:
Scenario B
The roommate asked your father to move ASAP. This puts you in a state confusion. Your father feels defeated, but puts on a brave face for your sake. You gently say: "It's okay, Dad. You have to be more careful in choosing a roommate next time." Taking a deep breath and hugging each other, your father says, "That's life. Something good will come out of it. I don't know how; I just know it will. I'll start looking for another place to live." You grab your backpack, look through the window and see your bus for school coming down the street. You hug your father as you both leave out of the house. He turns and smiles. You get your bus and arrive 5 minutes early to school and cheerfully greet the teacher.

Notice the difference?
Two different scenarios. Both started the same. Both ended different.
WHY? Because of how you reacted.

In the real world, you really have no control over 10% of what happens in your life.
The other 90% is determined by your reaction.
Here are some ways to apply the 10/90 principle:

❖ If someone says something negative about you, do not be a sponge. Let the attack roll off you like water on glass. You do not have to let the negative comments infect you. React properly and it will not ruin your day. A wrong reaction could result in losing a friend, being fired, being written up or getting stressed out.

❖ How do you react if someone cuts you off in the traffic? Do you lose your temper? Pound on the steering wheel? (a friend of mine once had the steering wheel fall off) Do you curse? Does your blood pressure skyrocket? Who cares if you arrive 10 seconds later to work? Why let the cars ruin your drive? Remember the 10/90 principle and don't worry about it.

❖ You are told you lost your job, did not get promoted, etc. Why lose sleep and get irritated? It will work out. Use your worrying energy and time to find a new job, study harder for a test or whatever the case might be.

❖ The plane is late. It is going to mangle your schedule for the day. Why take out your frustration on the flight attendant? She has no control over what is going on. Use your time to study, get to know the other passengers – why stress out? It will just make things worse. Now you know the 10/90 principle. Apply it and you will be amazed at the results. You will lose nothing if you try it.

The result? You will see it yourself.

Millions of people are suffering from undeserved stress, trials, problems and headaches. Bad days follow bad days. Terrible things seem to be constantly happening. There is a lack of joy and broken relationships. Worry consumes time. Anger breaks friendships, friends are lost, life seems dreary, and is not enjoyed to the fullest. If this seems like you, do not be discouraged. You can be different. Apply and understand the 10/90 principle. It will change your life.

Remember, we cannot control everything that happens to us, but we can control how we react to it. Everything we do, give, say or even think is like a **Boomerang**. It will come back to us.

10/90 PRINCIPLE
WORKSHEET

SITUATION: _____
_____
_____

HOW I REACTED: _____
_____
_____

WHAT HAPPENED: _____
_____
_____

SITUATION REVISTED:

HOW I COULD HAVE REACTED: _____
_____
_____

WHAT COULD HAVE HAPPENED IF I REACTED DIFFERENTLY: _____
_____
_____

LESSON 5

HANDLING THE UPS & DOWNS OF LIFE
Believe in your destiny; You are here for a reason.
I know the plans I have for you… plans to give you a hope and a future. Jeremiah 29:11

DO NOT
Allow negative experiences to make you bitter.
They should make you better & wiser.
And with that wisdom, you shall find
JOY!

SOMETIMES, YOU JUST HAVE TO
BOW YOUR HEAD, SAY A PRAYER,
AND WEATHER THE STORM.

When you can't control what's happening, challenge yourself to control how you respond to what's happening. That's where your power lies.

Not all storms come to disrupt your life, some come to clear your path.

Being a female is a matter of birth. being a woman is a matter of age. but being a lady is a matter of choice.

THE ONLY TIME YOU SHOULD LOOK BACK IS TO SEE HOW FAR YOU'VE COME.

Family is like
music,
some high notes,
some low notes,
but always a
beautiful song

There comes a time when you have to stop crossing oceans for people who wouldn't even jump puddles for you.

Life is an echo.
What you send out – comes back.
What you sow – you reap.
What you give – you get.
What you see in others – exists in you.
Do not judge - so you will not be judged.
Radiate and give love and love will come back to you.

Surround yourself with people who know your worth. You don't need too many people to be happy, just a few real ones who appreciate you for exactly who you are.

CHAPTER 6

PLACE SEEDS IN THE MIX,
THEN IN A CONTAINER IN ORDER TO GERMINATE.

LESSON 6

LESSON OUTLINE

AND

SAMPLE ACTIVITIES

LESSON 6: CONFLICT RESOLUTION – DECONSTRUCTING DISAGREEMENTS

FOUNDATIONAL TRUTH:
They sharpen their tongues like swords and aim cruel words like deadly arrows.   Psalms 64:3

LESSON OF THE SESSION:
Stick & stones may break my bones but words can never hurt me!
Stop, think, act! Words become memories;
memories become the soundtrack that is played in the mind over and over.

DEIRDRE-ISM
You can't make people respect you, however,
you don't have to be present for the disrespect – you can be disrespected in absentia.

IMPORTANT NOTE:
Words matter! The saying "sticks and stones may break my bones, but words will never hurt me" is an absolute lie! While words cannot break your bones, words can break your spirit and create in you a negative view of life. Bones can be set in a cast and be fused back together. However, words, once spoken, cannot be unsaid nor unheard, and can remain in the brain, on a continuous loop. Words form memories that continue to come forth when similar situations happen. Memories of positive affirmations build you up. Memories of negative criticism tear you down. What comes out of your mouth matters. What you tell yourself about yourself matters.

Words are a major source of communication. It is critical that the message that you send is the message that is received. Great misunderstandings happen when words are not received as they were intended. That is why it is important to think before you speak and to watch your words. When you understand this, you will learn that while you can't make anyone respect you, you do not have to be present for their disrespect – you

can be disrespected in absentia (without being there).

SUMMARY OF ACTIVITIES:
The activities will teach you about disagreements and how to work them out in a positive way. Activities will reveal aspects of disagreements, how anger affects, and how to successfully handle them.

LESSON SUMMARY:
You will learn about disagreements and how to prevent them from escalating into arguments, fights, and worse. Disagreements will be deconstructed and broken down into the steps that lead to escalation. De-escalation and conflict resolution strategy will be learned in order to positively resolve anger and disagreements. You will also learn that how you say your words (tone, body language, etc.) is as important as what you say. The lesson concludes with the Conflict Resolution/Bullying inspiration cards and poster.

LESSON 6   CONFLICT RESOLUTION –
DECONSTRUCTING DISAGREEMENTS

ICE BREAKER: TWO TRUTHS AND A LIE
This an activity where the participants share some truths about themselves and a lie.
The trick is to make the lie as convincing as the truth statement. This demonstrates
the importance of how you communicate what you say – does the lie sound like the truth
or does the truth sound like a lie???

Two Truths & A Lie
Hand out index cards and pencils to everyone in the group.
Have each person write down two truths and one lie on the card.
Each person takes a turn to share their card.
The person who guesses the lie, gets to go next.

LESSON 6

CONFLICT RESOLUTION/DISAGREEMENTS
Stick & stones may break my bones but words can never hurt me!
They sharpen their tongues like swords and aim cruel words like deadly arrows.   Psalms 64:3

Icebreaker: Two Truths and a Lie;

Reflection: Share a problem that you used the SODA method to help you resolve it.
Today I feel _____ because _____

Lesson of the Session: Stop/Think/Act!

Deirdre-ism: You can't make people respect you, however,
you don't have to be present for the disrespect – you can be disrespected in absentia.

Disagreements and Conflicts:
What is a disagreement/conflict? _____
What is the highest level of conflict/disagreement? _____
Share a recent disagreement that you had, with whom you had it with, and how it ended?
_____

Activities:
1. Deconstructing Disagreements & Conflicts
2. Handling Disagreements
3. Handling Disagreement Worksheet
    a. Understanding Disagreements
    b. Handling Disagreements Wisely
    c. Stopping Disagreements From Turning Into Arguments and Fights
4. Verbal Bullying ▶ https://www.youtube.com/watch?v=f-g-GuP748k - Elementary
5. Verbal Bullying ▶ https://www.youtube.com/watch?v=FlG6YtH3Z5c - Secondary
6. Inspiration Cards

Lesson of the session:
_____
_____

Something I learned:
_____
_____

Other things I thought about:
_____
_____

Lesson 6

DECONTRUCTING DISAGREEMENTS & CONFLICTS
(CONFLICT RESOLUTION)

What is a disagreement, conflict?
Disagreement per dictionary.com: Fail to agree; dissent, quarrel
Conflict per dictionary.com: Fight, battle, struggle; quarrel

LEVELS OF DISAGREEMENT/CONFLICT:

1. Not agreeing
2. Raising voices
3. Not listening to the other person
4. In your face yelling/shouting
5. Arguing

6. Pushing/shoving
7. Fighting
8. Friends joining in
9. Mob violence (riots, Jan. 6, 2021)
10. War

How do disagreements/conflicts make you feel?
What you do to protect your feelings (defense mechanisms) ?
(deny – "that's not true", lie – "I don't care", etc.)

What are some conflicts/disagreements that you have and with whom?

_____
_____

Behavior that goes with the levels of disagreement/conflict:

_____
_____

What do you do (what is your behavior) when you disagree with a
Friend _____
Sibling _____
Parent _____
Teacher _____
Police _____
Other _____

HANDLING DISAGREEMENTS

What is a disagreement? A disagreement is what happens when people do not agree or do not have the same opinion on something. Because people are different and have different experiences, there are going to be disagreements.

That is a fact of life. However, disagreements do not have to lead to arguments, fights or worse. By understanding disagreements and learning how to handle them wisely, you will be able to stop them from escalating to arguments, fights or worse.

UNDERSTANDING DISAGREEMENTS

1. It is okay to disagree – people are different, have different experiences, have different likes and dislikes.
2. Because someone disagrees with you, they are not weird, bad, strange, etc. You do not agree.
3. If someone disagrees with your ideas, that doesn't mean that their ideas are not important or dumb. It means that their idea is different from yours.
4. When people disagree, that doesn't mean one is right and the other is wrong. It's possible that both could be right, both could be wrong, both could be partially right and partially wrong.
5. Disagreements do not have to end with both people agreeing. It is okay to agree to disagree.
6. Disagreements do not mean that the people disagreeing are mad at or dislike each other. You can disagree and still be friends.

HOW TO HANDLE DISAGREEMENTS WISELY

1. Figure out what the disagreement is about.
2. Listen to the other person to find out why they feel the way they do.
3. Share with the other person, why you feel the way you do.
4. Get the facts on both sides of the opinions.
5. Review the pros and cons and decide, together, what to do.
6. Implement what you decide to do.

PREVENTING DISAGREEMENTS FROM TURNING INTO AGRUEMENTS & FIGHTS

1. If you're tired, in a bad mood, or hangry (hunger makes one angry), do not get into discussion.
2. Make sure those you interact with have the same values, standards, rules as you.
3. If you have been wrong, admit it, apologize for it and mean it.
4. Respect other points of view, even if you do not agree with it.
5. Do not share your thoughts or opinions with those who do not accept or respect you.

HANDLING DISAGREEMENTS WORKSHEET

===

HANDLING DISAGREEMENTS WISELY

Write about a recent disagreement you had:

Who was the disagreement with? _____

What was the disagreement about? _____

Write how you felt about it? _____

Did you share how you felt with the person you disagreed with? _____ Yes _____ No

What are the facts, pros and cons, for your opinion?

1. _____

2. _____

3. _____

What are the facts, pros and cons, for the other person's opinion?

1. _____

2. _____

3. _____

What are the best pros for which opinion?

_____

_____

What's the best decision?

_____

_____

===

PREVENTING DISAGREEMENTS FROM ESCALATING

At the end of a very long day, a very important decision needs to be made. What do you do?

_____

You have a disagreement with someone who does not follow the same rules as you. What do you do?

_____

You realize that you were wrong about something you. What do you do?

_____

You have an opinion that is different than a good friend. What do you do?

_____

Someone you don't know is very negative and disrespectful towards your opinions. What do you do?

_____

LESSON 6

CONFLICT RESOLUTIONS/DISAGREEMENTS
Sticks & stones may break my bones but words can never hurt me.
They sharpen their tongues like swords and aim cruel word like deadly arrows. Psalms 64:3

WATCH YOUR THOUGHTS, FOR THEY BECOME WORDS.
WATCH YOUR WORDS, FOR THEY BECOME ACTIONS.
WATCH YOUR ACTIONS, FOR THEY BECOME HABITS.
WATCH YOUR HABITS, FOR THEY BECOME CHARACTER.
WATCH YOUR CHARACTER, FOR IT BECOMES YOUR DESTINY.

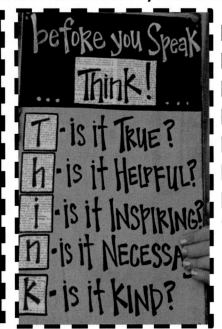

before you Speak ... Think! ...

T - is it TRUE?
h - is it HELPFUL?
i - is it INSPIRING?
n - is it NECESSAR
K - is it KIND?

Words and hearts should be handled with care. Words when spoken and hearts when broken are the hardest things to repair.

"Whoever is trying to bring you down is already below you."

Be very careful about what you think... Your thoughts run your life.

The tongue has no bones, but is strong enough to break a heart. So be careful with your words.

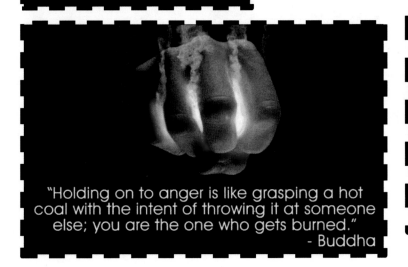

"Holding on to anger is like grasping a hot coal with the intent of throwing it at someone else; you are the one who gets burned."
- Buddha

10% of conflicts are due to difference in opinion.
90% are due to wrong tone of voice.

97

CHAPTER 7

COVER WITH A PLASTIC LID
THAT ALLOWS LIGHT THROUGH BUT HOLDS MOISTURE IN.

LESSON 7

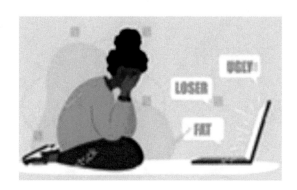

LESSON OUTLINE

AND

SAMPLE ACTIVITIES

LESSON 7: CONFLICT RESOLUTION: CYBERBULLYING/ SOCIAL-MEDIA

FOUNDATIONAL TRUTH:
Death and life are in the power of the tongue, and those who love it will eat its fruit.   Proverbs 18:21

LESSON OF THE SESSION:
Sticks & stones may break my bones, but words stay with me forever!
What goes in cyberspace, stays in cyberspace.
Think before you post!

DEIRDRE-ISM:
When people show you who they are, believe them. Maya Angelou

IMPORTANT NOTE:
Words are very important. They leave you with lifelong memories. When you are struggling to accomplish something, you will remember the words of the significant people in your life – parents, grandparent, teachers, family members, etc. Do you hear encouraging words like "you can do whatever you put your mind to" or do you hear discouraging words like "you're never gonna amount to anything"? The words you remember make a monumental difference because the memories will either build you up or tear you down.

In this day of social media, you must be careful navigating social media platforms. Not only because of adults preying on children and teens, but also because what you post online will stay in cyberspace forever! You may not believe it, but it is true. You may share some very personal pictures or thoughts with your "boo". They promised that they would keep it between just the two of you. Then your friendship changes and your thoughts and pictures end up on multiple social media platforms for all the world to see, FOREVER!!!

So, you must think before you share and post on social media because it can come back to

harm you. Real life examples of consequences of posting on social media:
- People on disability (injured and unable to work) posting their activities on Facebook, get terminated from their disability payments because the posted pictures show no evidence of disability in their activities.
- Parents had sued their daughter's school and won a substantial financial settlement with the condition that the amount would not be disclosed. Their daughter posted the amount of the settlement on Facebook; the school found out which caused the parents to forfeit and had to return what had been paid.
- Many people have lost jobs due to the posting of racist rants and antics (Karens'). Be very thoughtful when using social media. Stop and think before you post on social media. When people show you who they are, believe them. And remember, you do not have be present for abuse and disrespect.

SUMMARY OF ACTIVITIES:
The activities will explore the presence and influence of social media, focusing on cyberbullying. What can you do? How do you react? Realistic, easy to implement strategies and solutions will be given.

LESSON SUMMARY:

Think about the reactions your words will create before you speak, write, or post. You can learn great lessons from the things you don't get the chance to correct. Here some things you never get back:

- Words that have been spoken. Words, once said, can never be taken back, can never be unheard. So always think before you speak.
- The stone that's been thrown. It's easy to judge others, but judgment has a way of turning on us—and you find yourself someday misunderstood.
- The deed after it is done. Once you do something, you cannot undo it.
- The word after it is written (posted). Once it's written or posted in cyberspace, it stays there. Screenshots keep it alive and well.
- Time – You can't hold it or save it. It's your choice either to use it or waste it.
- Moments after they are missed. Time waits for no one.
- Opportunity that is missed. If you do not take an opportunity when you have the chance, you will never get back that same opportunity.
- Trust – It has the power to bond people. Once a trust is broken, it is gone.

The lesson concludes with the Conflict Resolution – Cyberbullying/Social Media inspiration cards and poster

LESSON 7   CONFLICT RESOLUTION:
CYBERBULLYING/ SOCIAL-MEDIA

ACTIVITY: ICE BREAKER - TEETH

Everyone sits in a circle. Each player chooses a fruit or vegetable. The first player says their fruit or vegetable twice. Then the next player says the previous player's fruit/vegetable and adds their fruit/vegetable onto it, and so on. Player A says strawberry strawberry; player B says strawberry strawberry, broccoli broccoli; player C says strawberry strawberry, broccoli broccoli, carrot carrot, etc. until the last player says has her turn.

What makes this game fun is that you can't show your teeth at any point (which you do by pulling your lips over your teeth). If you do happen to show your teeth and get caught by anyone, you alert the group by screaming "teeth teeth" and flapping your arms at the player like wings (making sure you don't show your teeth in the process!). when teeth are shown, the person is eliminated from the game.

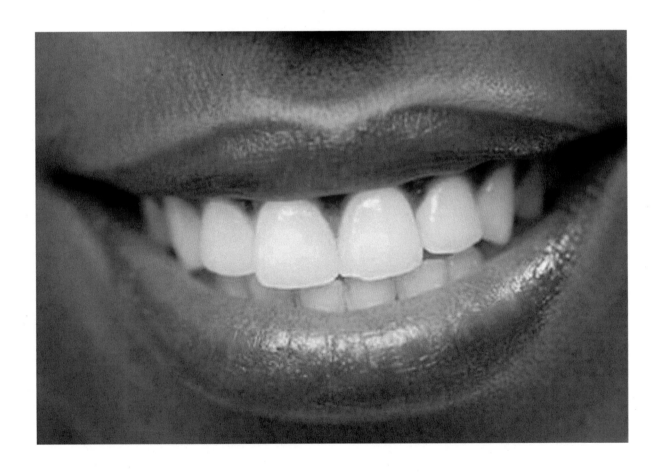

ELEMENTARY
LESSON 7

CONFLICT RESOLUTION: CYBERBULLYING/SOCIAL MEDIA
Sticks & stones can break my bones, but words stay with me forever!
Death and life are in the power of the tongue, and those who love it will eat its fruit.   Proverbs 18:21

Icebreaker: Teeth
Reflection: Name a disagreement/conflict that you had this week. Share how you handled it.
Lesson of the Session: What goes in cyberspace, stays in cyberspace.
Deirdre-ism: When people show you how they are – believe them. Maya Angelou

Social Media – Help or Harm?

Pros:
- get information quickly
- keep you connected to people
_____
_____

Cons:
- wrong information spreads rapidly
- write what you would not say face to face
- unfiltered words and thoughts
_____

How do disagreements/conflicts manifest today? _____
_____
How do you handle disagreements on social media? _____
_____

Social Media
1. Social-Media/Cyberbullying Safety sheet
2. Think Before You Post: ▶ https://www.youtube.com/watch?v=J6PuMw3YjD0
Remember, screenshots keep deleted messages going on and on and on and on.

Bullying:
1. Red Hair Boy Bullied: ▶ https://www.youtube.com/watch?v=nWJut7KQhI4

Cyberbullying:
1. News Anchor Bullied, Message to Her Bully: ▶ https://www.youtube.com/watch?v=QW6CNTXqBCM

Cyber Safety:
1. Do You Know Who You're Talking To?: ▶ https://www.youtube.com/watch?v=DZ_f7yOAzPU
2. MySpace, A Must Read*: 📶 https://www.badgerandblade.com/forum/threads/myspace-a-must-read-for-all.21158/   *insert latest social media platform

Inspiration Cards

Lesson of the session: _____

Something I learned: _____

Other things I thought about: _____

CONFLICT RESOLUTION/CYBERBULLYING
Sticks & stones can break my bones, but words stay with me forever!
Death and life are in the power of the tongue, and those who love it will eat its fruit.   Proverbs 18:21

Icebreaker: Teeth
Reflection: Name a disagreement/conflict that you had this week. Share how you handled it.
Lesson of the session: What Goes in Cyberspace Stays In Cyberspace.
Deirdre-ism: When people show you who they are – believe them. Maya Angelou

Social Media – Help or Harm?

Pros:
- get information quickly
- keep you connected to people
- _____
- _____

Cons:
- wrong information spreads rapidly
- write what you would not say face to face
- unfiltered words and thoughts
- _____

Cyberbullying via social media – How do disagreements/conflicts manifest today?
_____

Cyberbullying – How do you handle disagreements on social media?
_____

Social Media: Think Before You Send
- ▶ https://www.youtube.com/watch?v=ObHyjhS4BZw e
- ▶ https://www.youtube.com/watch?v=BcdZm3WAF4A
- ▶ https://www.youtube.com/watch?v=tal2MP7Uo1k

Screenshots keeps delete messages going on and on and on and on and ….

Cyberbullying
- ▶ News Anchor Bullied- Her Reply: https://www.youtube.com/watch?v=QW6CNTXqBCM

Cyber Safety:
Online Safety Tips
- ▶ MySpace, A Must Read*(*insert latest social media):
- ⓕ https://www.badgerandblade.com/forum/threads/myspace-a-must-read-for-all.21158/
- ▶ Do You Know Who You're Talking To? https://www.youtube.com/watch?v=IUjwHPah72o
- ▶ Amanda Todd Inspired Story https://www.youtube.com/watch?v=fmRo2cS2scU

Lesson of the session: _____

Something I learned: _____

Other things I thought about: _____

CYBERBULLYING AND SOCIAL MEDIA
STOP/THINK/ACT: WHAT GOES IN CYBERSPACE STAYS IN CYBERSPACE

Social Media Safety:
1. Talk with parents about rules (time and sites you are allowed to use)
2. Remember that nothing in social media is completely private.
3. Most Internet Service Providers have rules about online behavior.
4. Limit social media use. What is your balance between online and in-person activities?
5. Never share private information about others.
6. never say things that might violate the safety of others (even joking)
7. Do not share personal informant online – name, school name, address, phone number, and personal photos in places where strangers can find them.
8. _Never_ share passwords, account IDs, PINs with others (even your best friend), except your parents
9. Avoid chatting with strangers because people can be dishonest with their identity.
10. _NEVER_ send your picture/personal information to someone you only know online.
11. _NEVER_ meet an online friend in person without a parent's/guardians knowledge.
12. Do not open messages or attachments from people you don't know.

SOCIAL MEDIA BULLYING - WHAT TO DO:
1. Don't respond to bullying or inappropriate messages, but save them as evidence.
2. Block the email addresses and cell phones of people who are sending unwanted messages
3. Discuss the incidents that make you feel uncomfortable with a trusted adult (parents, teacher, or school counselor)
4. Always report online bullying, hate incidents, inappropriate sexual activity and threats of harm to self or others to adult family members (such as a parent), school authorities and police.
5. File complaints with service providers – Internet Services Providers, web sites, cell phone companies, etc. They can find the offenders, cancel their service, and report them to the police.
6. When in doubt about what to do, log off and ask for help from a trusted adult.

WITNESSING BULLYING:

* Take action!
* Take a stand!
* Don't join in to hurt someone!
* Don't encourage it!
* Report it!
* Be a friend!

LESSON 7

CONFLICT RESOLUTION/CYBERBULLYING

Sticks & stones can break my bones, but words stay with me forever!

Death and life are in the power of the tongue, and those who love it will eat its fruit. Proverbs 18:21

Problems are like washing machines. They twist, they spin & knock us around. But in the end we come out cleaner, brighter & better than before.

BEING HONEST MAY NOT GET YOU A LOT OF FRIENDS BUT IT'LL ALWAYS GET YOU THE RIGHT ONES.

— John Lennon

The problem with closed-minded people is that their mouth is always opened.

Today's Reality

Big House _____ Small Family
More Degrees _____ Less Common Sense
Advanced Medicine _____ Poor Health
Touched Moon _____ Neighbours Unknown
High Income _____ Less Peace of Mind
High IQ _____ Less Emotions
Good Knowledge _____ Less Wisdom
Number of Affairs _____ No True Love
Lot of Friends on Facebook _____ No Best Friends
More Alcohol facebook.com/learningpetals Less Water
Lots of Human _____ Less Humanity
Costly Watches _____ But No Time

You need to associate with people that inspire you, people that challenge you to rise higher, people that make you better. Don't waste your valuable time with people that are not adding to your growth. Your destiny is too important.

— JOEL OSTEEN

When you can't control what's happening, challenge yourself to control how you respond to what's happening. That's where your power lies.

Sometimes..

Just being there IS enough.

CHAPTER 8

WHEN THEY BEGIN SPROUTING, REMOVE THEIR COVER.

LESSON 8

LESSON OUTLINE

AND

SAMPLE ACTIVITIES

LESSON 8: PERSONAL STYLE, SOCIAL GRACE, & SOCIAL-MEDIA

FOUNDATIONAL TRUTH:
As a ring of gold in a swine's snout, so is a lovely woman who lacks discretion.
Proverbs 11:22

LESSON OF THE SESSION:
You never get a second chance to make a first impression!

DEIRDRE-ISM:
People will forget what you said and what you did.
But people will never forget how you made them feel. Maya Angelou

IMPORTANT NOTE:
While what you say is important, but *how* you say it is just as important. What you do is important, *how* you do it is just as important. In many instances, how you say or do something is reacted to more than the words or accomplishment. If someone compliments you with a scowl on their face, in an angry tone, do you respond to the words coming out of the mouth or to the way they look and sound? What we think and believe guides us through this thing called life, just as a map (oops, showing my age 😫), I mean, Waze, Google Drive, MapQuest, or any driving app, guides you to an unknow destination. It is the lens through which we chart our path and view our world.

How you carry yourself – how you talk, act, and react – is the focus of the lesson. You have discovered a lot about who you are, who you are accountable to, who influences you, what you like and dislike, your strengths and weaknesses, and what your talents are. Now you will begin to explore how you want to put all that together to show yourself to the world in an authentic, unique style that you are comfortable with. Remember, you are figuring things out. You have the right to change anything that makes you uncomfortable. You are learning, growing, developing into your future self. Some things will fit and some will not. And that is okay. Growing and developing is a process. Stay true to your beliefs and

thoughts because what you believe and think is best for you is your real living standard. People will forget what you said or did, but they will never forget how you made them feel.

SUMMARY OF ACTIVITIES:
The activities will take a real look at social media, the pros and cons, its perceptions, misperceptions. Knowing who you are, whose you are, who you're accountable to and considering the benefits and drawbacks of social media, you will learn the best way to navigate it for you.

LESSON SUMMARY:
Please know that marketing companies, influencers make money off of your dissatisfaction with yourself. Media plants seeds of dissatisfaction. Magazines photoshop models, social media apps have filters – all sending the message that you are not enough the way you are. This causes you to be dissatisfied with yourself no matter what. If you're light you wanna be darker, if you're dark you wanna be lighter; if you got a big breasts you want small ones, if got small breasts you want big ones; if you got big thighs you want little thighs, if you got little thighs you want big thighs; if you got curly hair you want straight hair, if you got straight hair you want curly hair; on and on. Don't be fooled – love being you boo! The lesson concludes with the Personal Style, Social Grace & Social Media inspiration cards and poster.

111

LESSON 8   PERSONAL STYLE, SOCIAL GRACE, & SOCIAL-MEDIA

ICE BREAKER: IF

This is a simple icebreaker to get young people talking and listening to others in the group. Ask the group to sit in a circle. Write 20 'IF' questions on cards and place them (question down) in the middle of the circle. The first person takes a card, reads it out and gives their answer, comment or explanation. The card is returned to the bottom of the pile before the next person takes their card. Keep it moving and don't play for too long. Write your own additional 'IF' questions to add to the list.

1. If you could go anywhere in the world, where would you go?
2. If I gave you $100,000, what would you spend it on?
3. If you could watch your favorite movie now, what would it be?
4. If you could talk to anyone in the world, who would it be?
5. If you could wish one thing to come true this year, what would it be?
6. If you could live in any period of history, when would it be?
7. If you could change anything about yourself, what would you change?
8. If you could be someone else, who would you be?
9. If you could have any question answered, what would it be?
10. If you could watch your favorite TV show now, what would it be?
11. If you could have any kind of pet, what would you have?
12. If you could do your dream job 10 years from now, what would it be?
13. If you had to be allergic to something, what would it be?
14. If you sat down next to Jesus on a bus, what would you talk about?
15. If money and time was no object, what would you be doing right now?
16. If you had one day to live over again, what day would you pick?
17. If you could eat your favorite food now, what would it be?
18. If you could learn any skill, what would it be?
19. If you were sent to live on a space station for three months and only allowed to bring three personal items with you, what would they be?
20. If you could buy a car right now, what would you buy?

LESSON 8

PERSONAL STYLE, SOCIAL GRACE, & SOCIAL MEDIA
You never get a 2nd chance to make a 1st impression
As a ring of gold in a swine's snout, so is a lovely woman who lacks discretion. Proverbs 11:22

Icebreaker: If...

Reflection: How does your preferred social media platform make you feel?

Lesson of the Session: You never get a 2nd chance to make a 1st impression.

Deirdre-ism: People will forget what you said and what you did, but they will never forget how you made them feel. Maya Angelou

What is happening in your world? What is feeding your mind? Who influences you?
Family, friends, school, church, TV, movies, musical artists, social media, society, etc...
Influences and experience directly affect your thoughts.

Find your unique style; appearances speak volumes.
Watch your words and actions, think for yourself. Remember:
- Appearances announce you. This is the time to find your unique style.
- Begin to think for yourself. Watch your words and actions.
- Understand that how you look influences what others think about you.
- If you dress the part, don't be surprised when you're treated like you're dressed.
- It's not so much WHAT you say, but HOW you say it.
- To have your own style, you must know yourself and think for yourself.

Activities:
1. Video: Body Image
     https://www.youtube.com/watch?v=17j5QzF3kqE
2. Watch Your Thoughts Worksheet
3. Finding Your Personal Style Worksheet
    Pair up and each pair share their answers with the group.
4. What Impression Do You Leave?
5. Inspiration Cards

Lesson of the session:
_____
_____

Something I learned:
_____
_____

Other things I thought about:
_____
_____

WATCH YOUR THOUGHTS WORKSHEET

We live in a world of thought.
Our thoughts create our experiences, and so, we experience what we think.
It is the quality of our thoughts, that create the quality of our life.
When we're unhappy where we are in life, we seek to create change.
If you want to change the outside, you must first change the inside.
You must change the attention of your thoughts because
What you think directly influences how you feel.

Watch your thoughts.
for they become **words.**

What do you think about yourself?
_____
_____

Watch your words.
for they become **actions.**

What words do you use to describe yourself?
_____
_____

Watch your actions.
for they become **habits.**

How do I act/behave normally?
_____
_____

Watch your habits.
for they become **character.**

What do I regularly do?
_____
_____

Watch your character.
for they become **your destiny.**

What do I do when nobody's watching?
_____
_____

FINDING YOUR PERSONAL STYLE:

Pair up and answer these questions.
Each pair share their answers with the group.

What do you like about the way you look?

1. _____
2. _____
3. _____

What makes you stand out/distinguishes you from others?

1. _____
2. _____
3. _____

Do you feel like you have a good reputation? If yes, why?

_____
_____

If no, why not? _____

_____

What beliefs do you live by? _____

_____

How do you show your character and integrity? _____

_____
_____

What do you think people see when they look at you? _____

_____
_____

WHAT IMPRESSIONS ARE YOU LEAVING?
WHAT DO PEOPLE REMEMBER ABOUT YOU WHEN YOU ARE NOT THERE?

CHECK THE BOXES OF THE SENTENCES BELOW THAT BEST DESCRIBE YOU:

☐ 1. I think well of myself.

☐ 2. I do not let your opinion change mine.

☐ 3. I do the things that need to be done.

☐ 4. I do not help until asked.

☐ 5. I am respectful and respected.

☐ 6. I do not stay in disrespectful environments.

☐ 7. I do my best in all situations.

☐ 8. I am not a slacker.

☐ 9. I offer help to those in need.

☐ 10. I think about me first.

☐ 11. I am willing to share the things I have.

☐ 12. I hoard my things for my use only.

☐ 13. I think before I speak.

☐ 14. I say whatever comes into mind.

☐ 15. I am considerate of other's feelings.

☐ 16. I only consider my feelings.

☐ 17. I do my best to figure things out.

☐ 18. I appreciate what is done for me.

☐ 19. I ask for help when I need it.

☐ 20. I treat others as I would like to be treated.

WHAT IMPRESSION DO I LEAVE WITH OTHERS?

Write the number of each checked sentence above that matches the description of the statements below and you will have an idea of the impression you leave about yourself:

Confident – I do not need your approval for me to like myself. _____

Responsible – I take care of my things. _____

Helpful – I offer to help out. _____

Resourceful – I seek out help. _____

Standard – I have my rules that I live by. _____

Considerate – I think about others. _____

Selfish – I put myself first all the time. _____

Inconsiderate – I speak my mind without hesitation. _____

Hard worker – I do my best effort. _____

Thankful – I am grateful for the things I have. _____

LESSON 8

PERSONAL STYLE, SOCIAL GRACE, & SOCIAL MEDIA
You never get a 2nd chance to make a 1st impression.

As a ring of gold in a swine's snout, so is a lovely woman who lacks discretion.

Proverbs 11:22

A lot of the pain that we are dealing with are really only THOUGHTS.

"Believe what you think

Caution:
IF YOU HANG OUT WITH ME FOR TOO LONG I WILL BRAINWASH YOU INTO BELIEVING IN YOURSELF AND KNOWING YOU CAN ACHIEVE YOUR DREAMS.

Correct each other in *private*. **Defend** each other in *public* and **keep your personal business** off Facebook.

Time does not change people, time reveals the real face of people.

The more man meditates upon good thoughts, the better will be his world and the world at large.

Confucius

AS I LOOK BACK ON MY LIFE, I REALIZE THAT EVERY TIME I THOUGHT I WAS BEING **REJECTED** FROM SOMETHING GOOD, I WAS ACTUALLY BEING RE-DIRECTED TO SOMETHING BETTER.

Everybody isn't your friend.

Just because they hang around you and laugh with you doesn't mean they are your friend. People pretend well. At the end of the day, real situations expose fake people, so pay attention.

There comes a time in life, when you walk away from all the drama and people who create it. Surround yourself with people who make you laugh, forget the bad, and focus on the good. Love the people who treat you right. Pray for the ones who don't. Life is too short to be anything but happy. Falling down is part of life, getting back up is living.

CHAPTER 9

CONTINUE TO WATER AS NEEDED TO KEEP THE SOIL MOIST.

LESSON 9

LESSON OUTLINE

AND

SAMPLE ACTIVITIES

LESSON 9

GET WISDOM

FOUNDATIONAL TRUTH:
Listen to counsel and receive instruction that you may be wise in your latter days.   Proverbs 19:20

LESSON OF THE SESSION:
You only make the same mistake once; the second time, it's a choice.

DEIRDRE-ISM:
Be grateful for the haters in your life because they show you what not to be.

IMPORTANT NOTE:
If you find yourself making the same mistake over and over, with different people in similar situations, you have not learned the life lesson. When you learn the lesson, then and only then, will you be able to move on to the next lesson that needs to be learned. Learning from your mistakes is wisdom.

Wisdom not only comes from learning from the mistakes you make, it comes from watching and learning from others. It is also doing now what you will be happy with later. Saving for an expensive item instead of putting it on a credit card and incurring debt and interest (extra money you are charged to pay it off monthly). Studying for your test, instead of playing games on your phone or computer, resulting in your getting a good grade. Practicing your basketball shots instead of hanging with your friends resulting in your getting more game playing time. Wisdom comes from making good choices. Wisdom helps you to be grateful for the haters in your life because they show you what not to be.

SUMMARY OF ACTIVITIES:
The activities will explore ways to get wisdom – learning from our mistakes, learning from other's mistakes and following guidance. Steps to survive adolescence issues will be viewed through the lens of knowing your value, making better choices, and setting real living standards.

LESSON SUMMARY:
Our lives are determined by the choices we make:
Choose to be kind instead of mean.
Choose to be forgiving instead of hurting.
Choose to be loving instead of hating.
Choose to be responsible instead of blaming.
Choose to be healing instead of infecting.
Choose to be better instead of bitter.
It's your life, it's your choice!
The lesson concludes with the Get Wisdom inspiration cards and poster.

LESSON 9   GET WISDOM

ICE BREAKER: THREE THINGS IN COMMON

THREE THINGS IN COMMON
The participants are divided into groups of 3 or 4. Each group must find three things that they have in common with each other. The weirder those things are — the better. After 10 minutes each group announces the three things they have in common. Everyone votes to decide which group has the "weirdest" three things in common.

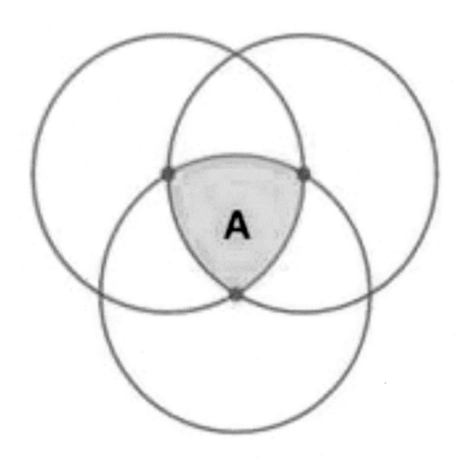

LESSON 9

GET WISDOM

You only make the same mistake once; the 2nd time, it's a choice.

Listen to counsel and receive instruction that you may be wise in your latter days.   Proverbs 19:20

Icebreaker: Three Things in Common

Review: What is your personal style?

Reflection: Share something that you did this week that was just you.

Lesson of the Session: Learn from your mistakes.

Deirdre-ism: Be grateful for the haters in your life because they show you how not to be.

Wisdom: Learning from your experiences/mistakes and from those of others;
Doing now what you will be happy with later.

Activities:
1. Getting Wisdom
2. Teen Survival Guide: https://www.in.gov/icw/files/teen_survival_guide1.pdf; p.40-60
   a. Feeling good about yourself
   b. Body image
   c. When you're not happy
   d. Taking charge of your world
   e. Healthy relationships
   f. Peer pressure & how to say no
   g. Dealing with bullies
   h. Staying Safe
3. Inspiration cards

Lesson of the session: _____

_____

Something I learned: _____

_____

Other things I thought about: _____

_____

Learning from your experiences, mistakes, and from others;
Doing now what you will be happy with later.

How to gain wisdom.

1. Try new things; don't be afraid of looking foolish. Write something new that you've tried.
_____

2. Learn from your mistakes. Write about a mistake you made and what you learned from it.
_____

3. Learn from others' mistakes. Write about something you learned from someone else's mistake.
_____

4. Know yourself, i.e., know who you are and whose you are.
. Write one thing you know about yourself
_____

5. Develop your own standards/rules for your life. Write one rule you have for yourself.
_____

6. Continue learning. Read, read, read. Write what you are interested in learning more about.
_____

7. Take care of your body, it's the only one you get. Write how you take care of your body.
_____

8. Converse with your elders – they are a wealth of experience and history. Ask a family elder to share their story. Write one thing they told you. _____

9. Develop your intuition. Intuition is that feeling in your gut that alerts you about, people or situations. Learn to trust it. Write about a time when you had a feeling in your gut.
_____
_____

10. Consider the consequences before you speak or act. Write about a time you thought before you acted. _____
_____

11. Delay gratification – sacrificing what you want now for what you want later (ex. doing extra chores so you can go to the place you want). Write about a time you delayed something you wanted to do.

_____
_____

12. Be willing to work for what you want, not taking the easiest way. Write about what you learned when you did not take a short cut. _____

_____

13. See the bigger picture – it's not just about you boo. Write about one thing you did for someone else. _____

_____

14. Be flexible and adaptable. Change is the only thing that is certain. Write about a time when you had to change your plan. _____

_____

15. Talk to people who are different from you and share a time you learned with others. Write one thing you learned from someone who is different from you. _____

_____

_____

To gain wisdom, you must learn from your experiences –
where you have gone, seen and done, who you have met and known –
and apply that to your life decisions in order to build a positive, productive life.

LESSON 9

GET WISDOM
You only make the same mistake once; the 2nd time, it's a choice.
Listen to counsel and receive instruction that you may be wise in your latter days. Proverbs 19:20

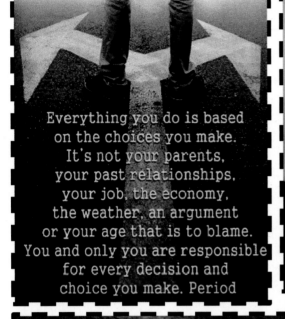

Everything you do is based
on the choices you make.
It's not your parents,
your past relationships,
your job, the economy,
the weather, an argument
or your age that is to blame.
You and only you are responsible
for every decision and
choice you make. Period

What is broken can be
mended. What hurts
can be healed. And no
matter how dark it
gets, the sun is going
to rise again.

We don't grow
when things are easy,
we grow when we face
challenges.
Unknown

It is during the worst times of your life
that you will get to see the true colors of
the people who say they care for you.
~Ritu Ghatourey

Remember,
being HAPPY
doesn't mean
you have it all.
It simply means
you're thankful
for all you have.

Wisdom:
doing now what we
will be happy with
later.

Though no one can go
back and make a
brand new start, anyone can
start from now and make a
brand new ending.

the PAST is where you
learned the lesson.
the FUTURE is where you
apply the lesson.
don't give up in the
MIDDLE.

CHAPTER 10

IN ABOUT SIX WEEKS, THE SEEDLINGS WILL BE READY TO TRANSITION INTO THE GARDEN.

LESSON 10

LESSON OUTLINE

AND

SAMPLE ACTIVITIES

LESSON 10

HEALTHY LIVING/BUILDING A SUPPORT SYSTEM

FOUNDATIONAL TRUTH:
Two are better than one, for if one falls, the other can help her up.   Ecclesiastes 4:9-12

LESSON OF THE SESSION:
Be rich in the things that count.

DEIRDRE-ISM:
Know why you do what you do.
Knowing the why will carry you through the discouraging times.

IMPORTANT NOTE:
Before a life can grow into anything, it must have the basic physiological needs (food, water, warmth, etc.) and safety needs (security and safety) met.   After physical and security needs, feeling loved is the main requirement for one to value oneself. When you know your value, you can set real life standards that will help you be more disciplined, determined, and dedicated to achieving your desires. Discipline and determination will enable you so you can make better choices. You will be better equipped to determine those people who can support you and add to your life rather than take from it. You will be equipped to make better choices whether it be healthy food, healthy living, or healthy relationships.

You will learn to seek to become rich in the things that count – food to eat, a place to sleep, love of family and friends, and a purpose in life. Knowing why you do what you do will carry you though the discouraging times.

SUMMARY OF ACTIVITIES:
The activities will have you evaluate relationships and life habits, choose relationships, and develop habits that will move you towards your life's interests, purposes, and goals.

LESSON SUMMARY:
All that glitters is not gold. And much disappointment comes with that realization. The goal of making money (being rich) turns out not to be all that people think it will be. It is an empty, lonely goal. There's a reason for the saying "It's lonely at the top". That's usually because of all the people that were stepped upon while making it to the top. How many famous people have killed themselves outright by suicide or by drug overdose? Too many. The real cost of being rich is being alone with yourself.

Being rich in the things that count builds supportive relationships and gives back to family, community, and society. It keeps us really connected to each other. What good is it to attain riches with no one who cares about you? So, strive to be rich in the things that count and you will have a life that's priceless! The lesson concludes with the Healthy Living/Building A Support System inspiration cards and poster.

LESSON 10   HEALTHY LIVING/
BUILDING A SUPPORT SYSTEM

ICE BREAKER: CREATE A STORY

Create a Story
The final activity is to create a story. Have one participant start a story. The person sitting next to her adds more to the story, and so on. The last person ends the story. By the end of the game, you have a very creative tale!

Once upon a time......

......and that's how the story

ends!

ELEMENTARY
LESSON 10

GETTING WISDOM/ BUILDING A SUPPORT SYSTEM
Be rich in the things that count.
Two are better than one, for if one falls, the other can help her up.   Ecclesiastes 4:9-12

Icebreaker: Create a Story
Review: What is wisdom?
Reflection: Share something wise that you did this week.
Lesson of the Session: We need real connections.
Deirdre-ism: Know the why of what you do; knowing the why will carry your through difficult times.

Getting Wisdom: Learning from your experiences/mistakes and from those of others;
Doing now what you will be happy with later.

Activities: 1. Building A Support System:
- Choosing A Friend/Being A Friend
- Making The Right Connections/Who Am I Connected To?
- Sometimes Adults Are Just Wrong
- Finding The Right Mentor

2. Setting Goals: What do you want to improve?
- In school
- Personal
- Behavior
- What's stopping you from improving?

3. Inspiration Cards

Lesson of the Session:

_____
_____

Something that I learned:

_____
_____

Other thoughts:

_____
_____

132

CHARACTERISTICS OF FRIENDSHIPS
What actions help friendships to form?

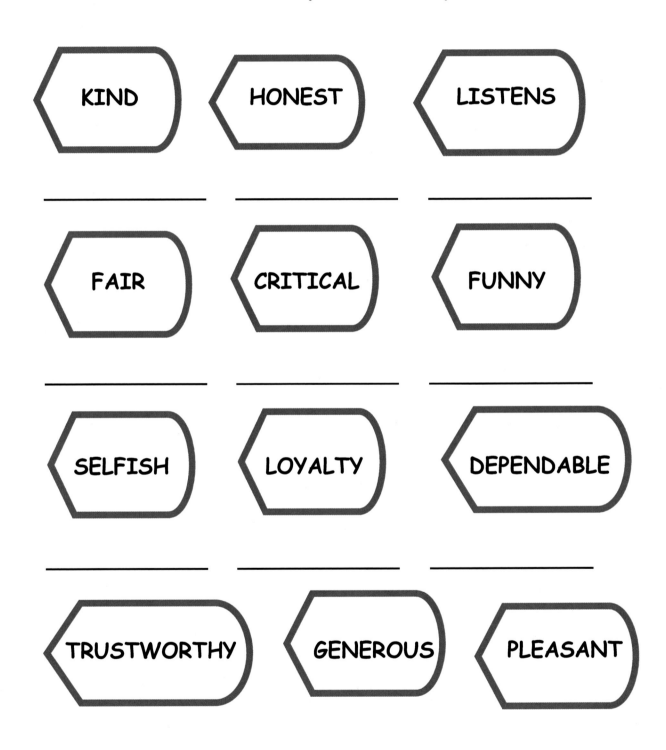

KIND

HONEST

LISTENS

FAIR

CRITICAL

FUNNY

SELFISH

LOYALTY

DEPENDABLE

TRUSTWORTHY

GENEROUS

PLEASANT

WHAT IS A FRIEND?

1. Tattles on you when you make a mistake.   __Y __N

2. Helps you when you are stuck.   __Y __N

3. Waits for you before going somewhere.   __Y __N

4. Lets you play with their toys sometimes.   __Y __N

5. Always wants to do things their way.   __y __N

6. Takes care of your pet when you go on vacation.   __Y __N

7. Uses your things without asking.   __Y __N

8. Stops you from getting into trouble.   __Y __N

9. Lets you borrow some things (with permission).   __Y __N

10. Cheers you up when you feel bad.   __Y __N

Making the right connections
Who am I connected to? Who do I count on?

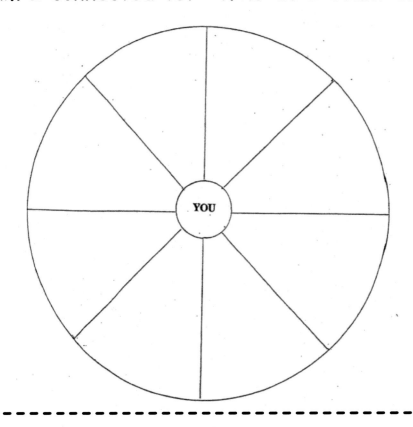

- -

Self-Advocacy Questions

1. What kind of help do I need?

   _____

2. What resources (people/things) can I use to get me help?

   _____

3. What phone numbers do I know by heart (memorized)?

   _____

4. Who can I talk to/go to when something is wrong?

   _____

SOMETIMES ADULTS ARE JUST WRONG!

Grownups are the ones that tell kids what is wrong and what is right. They make the rules that kids are to obey. They set the standard of how kids are to talk and behave. They set the standard of respect; how we are to respect others and ourselves. They say that we are to treat others the way we want to be treated. They say that kids are to speak kindly and respectfully. BUT….

Not all adults behave and speak the way they say kids should behave and speak.
Not all adults treat others the way that they want to be treated.
Not all adults speak kindly or respectfully.
And if they are called on it, the response is "Do as I say, not as I do".

Real examples of adults not doing the right thing include:
That teacher that makes fun of you/puts you down in front of the class;
That coach that calls you stupid because you didn't make the play;
That parent who says you're gonna be nothing, just like your dad/mom/_____ (fill in the blank);
That school counselor who says you won't get into your dream college;
That aunt/uncle/grandma/grandpa/other significant adult in your life tells you that you'll never make it to your goal because you are too lazy, too slow, too shy, too _____ (fill in the blank).
Write your own example of an adult you know that does not do the right thing:

_____

This poses a dilemma for kids.
1. How do you behave a in a way that you have never seen?
2. How do you achieve your goals when your teacher shoots you down?
3. How do you improve your skills if you are put down by the coach?
4. How do you stay motivated to be better when you are constantly compared to the one who failed?

While it may seem hopeless, it is not. There **ARE** things you can do to improve yourself, your skills, and your outlook, **IF** you really want to. How, you ask? By building a healthy support system, by surrounding yourself with trustworthy people (friends, relatives, teachers, scout leader, etc.) who show you by what they say and do, that they are for you. They encourage you to do the right things, to pursue your interests and goals, to be respectful, and treat others as you want to be treated.

List some people in your life that have proven themselves to be trustworthy:
Friends: _____   _____
_____   _____

Adults: _____   _____
_____   _____

Write how they have shown that they are on your side: _____
_____
_____

FINDING A MENTOR

Below is a fundamental list of character traits that a mentor should have. It is not all-inclusive. This list will give you an idea of what to look for when you are searching for a mentor.

- ☐ Trustworthiness –Have they have proven themselves worthy of trust with family and community?
- ☐ Availability – Do they have the time to commit to being involved?
- ☐ Positive behavior and speech – Have they modeled positive social skills and interpersonal relationships beyond family?
- ☐ Sensitivity – Are they able to gently share the truth, even it though it may hurt?
- ☐ Potential – Do they have the ability to see the potential in you that you may not see in yourself?
- ☐ Good listener – Do they listen before they respond?
- ☐ Provides support and encouragement – Are they able to help others overcome obstacles by helping them to problem solve?
- ☐ Challenge appropriately – Do they know how to challenge you without making you feel uncomfortable? Do they have the ability to help set expectations that enable their mentees to achieve more than what they thought possible?
- ☐ Non-judgmental/open minded. Do they limit imposing their beliefs and listen in a judgment-free zone? Are they able to assist in problem-solving and work through issues?
- ☐ Perspective/Wisdom – Adults have years of life experience; can they can give perspective to the perceived challenges of youth and assure them that they will get through what they are going through? Adults are like big rig trucks on the highway of life that can see far beyond the car in front of them. Youth are like compact cars that can only see the car in front and on the side of them.
- ☐ Sense of humor – Can they find the laughter/funny/light side of things?

Keep in mind that mentors give their time, energy, and effort for your benefit. You must come to the mentorship with, a cooperative mindset, a willingness to work, and an attitude of gratitude for the time someone has taken to invest in you.

MY GOALS

NAME: _____

DATE: _____

ACADEMIC GOALS
I will do the following to reach my goals:
1. _____
2. _____
3. _____
4. _____

WHAT'S STOPPING ME:
1. _____
2. _____
3. _____
4. _____
I will achieve this goal by _____

PERSONAL GOALS
I will do the following to reach my goals:
1._____
2. _____
3. _____
4. _____

WHAT'S STOPPING ME:
1. _____
2. _____
3. _____
4. _____
I will achieve this goal by _____

BEHAVIOR GOALS
I will do the following to reach my goals:
1. _____
2. _____
3. _____
4. _____

WHAT'S STOPPING ME:
1._____
2. _____
3. _____
4. _____
I will achieve this goal by _____

ATTENDANCE GOALS
I will do the following to reach my goals:
1. _____
2. _____
3. _____
4. _____

WHAT'S STOPPING ME:
1. _____
2. _____
3. _____
4. _____
I will achieve this goal by _____

HEALTHY LIVING/BUILDING A SUPPORT SYSTEM
Be rich in the things that count.
Two are better than one, for if one falls, the other can help her up.   Ecclesiastes 4:9-12

Icebreaker: Create a Story
Review: What is wisdom?
Reflection: Share something wise that you did this week.
Lesson of the Session: We need real connections.
Deirdre-ism: Know the why of what you do.
Knowing why you do what you do will carry you through the difficult times.

Activities: 1. Who Am I Connected To/Connection Wheel
2. Finding the Right Mentor
3. Getting Real/Keeping It 100
    a. Sometimes Adults Are Just Wrong.
    b. Advocating For Yourself
    c. Healthy vs Unhealthy Friendships/Relationships
    d. Exiting Unhealthy Friendships/Relationships
    e. Getting Your Priorities In Order

4. Setting Goals:
    a. Where am I now?
    b. Where do I want to be?
    c. What steps do I take to begin?
    d. What needs to be eliminated?
    e. What mistakes have I made?
    f. Where I plan to be in 2/4/6 months?

Lesson of the session:

_____

_____

Something I learned:

_____

_____

Other things I thought about:

_____

_____

Use the map below and write who you are connected to.
Who is there for you when you need help?
Make sure to write who they are to you – teacher, friend, relative, etc.

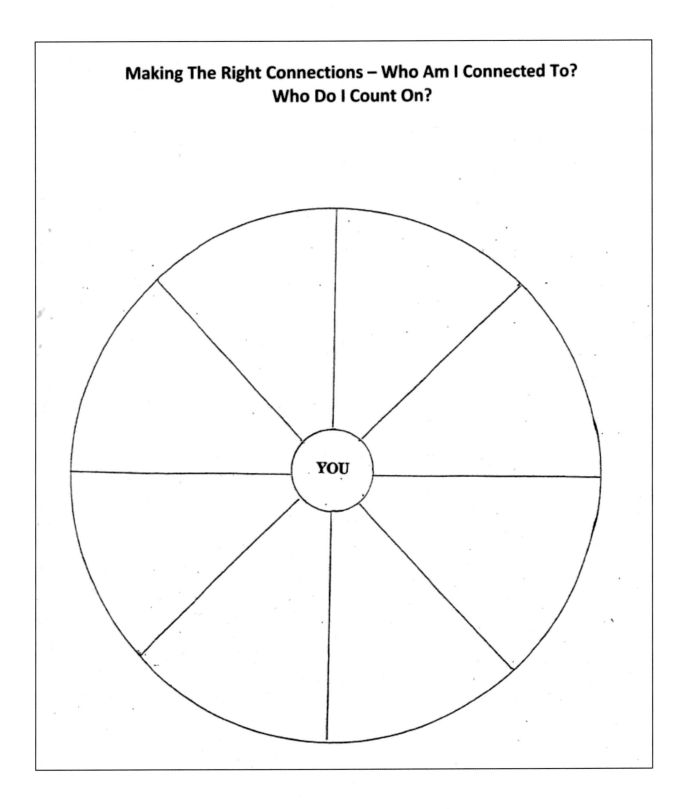

Making The Right Connections – Who Am I Connected To?
Who Do I Count On?

YOU

FINDING A MENTOR

Below is a fundamental list of character traits that a mentor should have. It is not all-inclusive. This list will give you an idea of what to look for when you are searching for a mentor.

- ☐ Trustworthiness – they have proven themselves worthy of trust with family and community.
- ☐ Availability – they have the time to commit to being involved.
- ☐ Positive behavior and speech – they model positive social skills and interpersonal relationships beyond family.
- ☐ Sensitivity – they are able to gently share the truth, even it though it may hurt.
- ☐ Potential – they have the ability to see the potential in you that you may not see in yourself.
- ☐ Good listener – they listen before they respond.
- ☐ Provides support and encouragement – they are able to help overcome obstacles by helping them to problem solve
- ☐ Challenge appropriately – they know how to challenge you without making you feel uncomfortable; has the ability to help set expectations enabling their mentees to achieve more than what they thought possible.
- ☐ Non-judgmental/open minded - limits imposing their beliefs and listens in a judgment-free zone, helping to problem-solve and work through issues.
- ☐ Perspective/Wisdom – Because adults have years of life experience, they can give perspective to the perceived challenges of youth and can assure them that they will get through what they are going through. Adults are like big rig trucks on the highway of life that can see far beyond the car in front of them. Youth are like compact cars that can only see the car in front and on the side of them.

Keep in mind that mentors give their time, energy, and effort for your benefit. You must come to the mentorship with, a cooperative mindset, a willingness to work, and an attitude of gratitude for the time someone has taken to invest in you.

SOMETIMES ADULTS ARE JUST WRONG!

Grownups are the ones that tell kids what is wrong and what is right. They make the rules that kids are to obey. They set the standard of how kids are to talk and behave. They set the standard of respect; how we are to respect others and ourselves. They say that kids are to treat others the way we want to be treated. They say that kids are to speak kindly and respectfully. BUT....

Not all adults behave and speak the way they say kids should behave and speak.
Not all adults treat others the way that they want to be treated.
Not all adults speak kindly or respectfully.
And if they are called on it, the response is "Do as I say, not as I do".

Real examples of adults not doing the right thing include:
That teacher that makes fun of you/puts you down in front of the class;
That coach that calls you stupid because you didn't make the play;
That parent who says you're gonna be nothing, just like your dad/mom/_____ (fill in the blank);
That school counselor who says you won't get into your dream college;
That aunt/uncle/grandma/grandpa/other significant adult in your life tells you that you'll never make it to your goal because you are too lazy, too slow, too shy, too _____ (fill in the blank). Write your own example of an adult you know that does not do the right thing:
_____

This poses a dilemma for kids.
1. How do you behave a in a way that you have never seen?
2. How do you achieve your goals when your teacher shoots you down?
3. How do you improve your skills if you are put down by the coach?
4. How do you stay motivated to be better when you are constantly compared to the one who failed?

While it may seem hopeless, it is not. There **ARE** things you can do to improve yourself, your skills, and your outlook, **IF** you really want to. How, you ask? By building a healthy, support system, by surrounding yourself with trustworthy people (friends, relatives, teachers, scout leader, etc.) who show you by what they say and do, that they are for you. They encourage you to do the right things, to pursue your interests and goals, to be respectful, and treat others as you want to be treated.

List some people in your life that have proven themselves to be trustworthy:
Friends: _____   _____
         _____   _____

Adults: _____   _____
         _____   _____

Write how they have shown that they are on your side: _____
_____
_____

ADVOCATE FOR YOURSELF!!!

ADVOCACY

Advocacy means to speak up for something. Self-advocacy means speaking up/sticking up for yourself.   In order to speak up for yourself, you must know the area where you need help. Below are some questions that will help you advocate for what you need.

1. What area do I need help?
2. Who can I trust and depend on to help me?
3. Have I memorized their contact information?
4. How many people's contact information do I have memorized?
5. What things (resources) do I need to help?
6. Do I know how to get the resource information?

Below, write about a problem you have or have had in the past and provide the answers to the advocacy questions above.

Problem: _____

_____

1._____

2._____

3._____

4._____

5._____

6._____

HEALTHY FRIENDSHIPS VS. UNHEALTHY FRIENDSHIPS

Friendship is at the heart of all relationships. It is foundation upon which relationships are built. Healthy friendships are characterized by trust, mutual respect and support, and good communication. This means that you can express your inner feelings without fear of being gossiped about; that you can expect support even if your goals are different from theirs; that your boundaries will be respected without fear of judgement or ridicule; that your feelings will be dealt with in a kind and compassionate way.

Healthy friendships encompass mutual trust, respect, understanding, honesty, and good communication.

Unhealthy friendships are one-sided relationships where the respect and balance is not mutual. Examples of one-sided friendships are if one person is always in charge, making all the decisions or if only one person is putting effort into the friendship.

Sometimes unhealthy friendships will involve mean, unkind, or passive aggressive behavior. Passive aggression is a type of indirect aggression that allows one person to express anger subtly in such a way that can be easily denied. It often involves inaction rather than action, such as the silent treatment. Other examples are being late, avoidance, subtle putdowns, and sarcasm (words used with the intention to hurt feelings). Some signs of unhealthy friendships are:
- There is more drama.
- Your friend is controlling. A friend who becomes extremely jealous and angry because you are spending time with a new person might not be a good friend to have.
- They get mad at you easily and a lot.
- They are pressuring you to do things you don't want to do or will get you in trouble.
- They are mean to you. There is big a difference between sharing your opinion and feelings and saying something that is intentionally hurtful.
- They are mean to others.

Unhealthy relationships need to be cut off. This can be done without being mean, cruel, or rude. First, slowly stop accepting behaviors that you used to readily take from your friend. Next, slowly stop accepting things from them. Then slowly, stop sharing the things in your life, good or bad, with them. Let some time pass and slip your news into the middle of a conversation, as if you've already told them. If they say anything, simply say that you thought you'd told them. Then become busy doing things they do not do. Finally, slow down your presence on social media.

In summary, positive friendships provide companionship, support, and a sense of belonging. They encourage and reinforce healthy behavior, like doing well in school. They help develop positive social skills, like cooperation, communication, conflict resolution, and resisting negative peer pressure. Finally, positive friendships in adolescence lay the groundwork for positive adult relationships.

HEALTHY RELATIONSHIP OR UNHEALTHY RELATIONSHIP

Think of your friendships. Each statement below describes an aspect of friendship. If the sentence describes a healthy friendship, check "H". If it describes an unhealthy friendship, check "U". Review where the majority of your checks are placed. Evaluate whether your friendships are healthy or unhealthy.

Your friend calls you several times a day and gets upset if you do not respond quickly. __H __U

Your friend listens to you and respects what you have to say. __H __U

Your friend doesn't want you to hang out with other friends. __H __U

When you disagree, your friend listens to what you have to say. __H __U

Your friend tells you to ignore what your parents say and ignore the rules they set. __H __U

Your friend encourages you to pursue your dreams and goals. __H __U

Your friend gets jealous when you talk with other people. __H __U

Your friend is honest and truthful with you. __H __U

Your friend puts you down and says negative things about you. __H __U

Your friend apologizes, and means it, when they are wrong or made a mistake. __H __U

Your friend pressures you to do things that you are not comfortable doing. __H __U

Your friend supports your interests like sports and extracurricular activities. __H __U

Your friend takes their bad mood out on you. __H __U

Your friend accepts responsibility for their behavior. __H __U

Your friend gets mad quickly when you disagree or say no to them. __H __U

Your friend allows you space if you need it. __H __U

Your friend makes all the decisions about what things you will do. __H __U

Your friend is not ashamed or embarrassed of your friendship. __H __U

Check the sentence that best described your answers:
Most of my friendships are healthy friendships. ____   Most of my friendships are unhealthy friendships. ____
Some of my friendships are healthy friendships. ____   Some of my friendships are unhealthy friendships. ____
Few of my friendships are healthy friendships. ____   Few of my friendships are unhealthy friedships.   ____

EXITING UNHEALTHY FRIENDSHIPS

SET BOUNDARIES/SET STANDARDS
A boundary is a barrier that limits how far one can go. Boundary is another wod for standard. Setting boundaries/setting standards with people is your way of letting people know how far they can go with you. It lets people know what is okay and what is not okay to do to you. To set your boundaries, you must.

1. Say what you mean so that others understand you.
2. Do not let other people's opinions change yours.
3. Stand for what is best for you.

If people keep crossing your boundaries, perhaps you should rethink the friendship. Ask yourself if the friendship is in my best insterest?

Once you know what your boundaries/standards are, it is easier to make a stand and hold your ground. To begin the exiting process, the following statements can be used:

- That is somethig I don't want to talk about.
- I don't like being called that name.
- You are making me uncomfortable. Please stop.
- I don't think that's funny. Please stop.
- That's not somethig I want to share about myself.
- I need you to respect what I said or else I'm going to leave.
- I don't allow people to treat me that way.

If people keep crossing your boundaries, maybe they shouldn't be your friend. Real friends respect and honor each other's boundaries.

GETTING MY PRIORITIES IN ORDER
WHAT IS IMPORTANT FOR ME
TO GROW AND THRIVE?

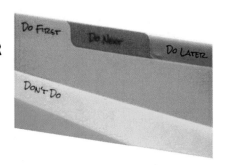

Answer the following questions honestly about your circle of friends.
It will tell whether your priorities are in good order for you to grow and thrive.

In my circle of friends:

Is there a spirit of envy and jealousy?	__yes __no
Is there rebellious activity?	__yes __no
Is there a type of control?	__yes __no
Is there a respect for school rules?	__yes __no
Is there respect for authority? (parents, teachers, elders, etc.)	__yes __no
Is there engagement in criminal activity? (FYI - ditching school is against the law)	__yes __no
Is there a sense of entitlement?	__yes __no
Is there an attitude of gratitude?	__yes __no
Is there an overall attitude of respect for people and property?	__yes __no
Do we have a good reputation?	__yes __no
Do we show that we care about others?	__yes __no
Do we try to do our best?	__yes __no
Are we encouraging?	__yes __no
Are we discouraging?	__yes __no
Do we see school as important?	__yes __no
Are we seen as positive?	__yes __no
Do we see our school and community as important?	__yes __no
Are we seen as disrespectful?	__yes __no

What are your priorities? (What is important to you)

_____

_____

How do your answers reflect your priorities?

_____

_____

_____

Do your answers show that you are doing those things that will help you achieve your priorities?
_____ Yes   _____No
If you checked yes, keep doing what you're doing! You're on the right track.
If you checked no, write what you can do to get on the right track to achieve your priorities.

_____

_____

MY GOALS

NAME: _____   **DATE:** _____

ACADEMIC GOALS
I will do the following to reach my goals:
1. _____
2. _____
3. _____
4. _____

WHAT'S STOPPING ME:
1. _____
2. _____
3. _____
4. _____
I will achieve this goal by _____

PERSONAL GOALS
I will do the following to reach my goals:
1. _____
2. _____
3. _____
4. _____

WHAT'S STOPPING ME:
1. _____
2. _____
3. _____
4. _____
I will achieve this goal by _____

BEHAVIOR GOALS
I will do the following to reach my goals:
1. _____
2. _____
3. _____
4. _____

WHAT'S STOPPING ME:
1. _____
2. _____
3. _____
4. _____
I will achieve this goal by _____

ATTENDANCE GOALS
I will do the following to reach my goals:
1. _____
2. _____
3. _____
4. _____

WHAT'S STOPPING ME:
1. _____
2. _____
3. _____
4. _____
I will achieve this goal by _____

LESSON 10

HEALTHY LIVING/BUILDING A SUPPORT SYSTEM
Be rich in the things that count.
Two are better than one, for if one falls, the other can help her up. Ecclesiastes 4:9-10

"If an egg is broken by an outside force, life ends. If broken by an inside force, life begins. Great things always begin from the inside."

Life is too short. Cut out negativity, forget gossip, forgive the people who hurt you. Spend your days with the people who are always there.

Be strong enough to stand alone, smart enough to know when you need help, and brave enough to ask for it.

-Ziad K. Abdelnour

Don't compare your life to others. There's no comparison between the sun and the moon. *They shine when it's their time*.

7 RULES OF LIFE

1. **SMILE**
IT ALWAYS WORKS OUT IN THE END!

2. **BE KIND**
YOU HAVE THE POWER TO MAKE PEOPLE FEEL GOOD!

3. **DON'T GIVE UP**
IF IT DOESN'T WORK THE FIRST TIME, FIND ANOTHER WAY!

4. **DON'T COMPARE**
EVERYONE'S ON A DIFFERENT JOURNEY!

5. **AVOID NEGATIVITY**
AVOID NEGATIVE THOUGHTS, SITUATIONS & PEOPLE!

6. **MAKE PEACE WITH YOUR PAST**
FOCUS ON BEING PRESENT & CREATING A BETTER FUTURE!

7. **TAKE CARE OF YOUR BODY & MIND**
ONE STRUGGLES TO SURVIVE WITHOUT THE OTHER!

WHEN SOMEONE SHOWS YOU WHO THEY ARE BELIEVE THEM THE FIRST TIME

MAYA ANGELOU

Maybe not tonight, not tomorrow or the next day, but *everything is going to be okay*.

SURROUND YOURSELF ONLY WITH PEOPLE WHO ARE GOING TO LIFT YOU HIGHER

just when the caterpillar thought the world was over, it became a butterfly...

-proverb

We don't grow when things are easy, we grow when we face challenges.

Unknown

150

CONCLUSION

Now that you have completed the G.I.R.L.S lessons:

You know you are valuable (lesson 1).
You know who you are, whose you are, and who you are accountable to (lesson 2).
This equips you to make better choices (lesson 3) and
Establish self-discipline and standards (lesson 4).
Now you are able to be more disciplined and make better choices.
This places you in a better position to handle the ups and downs of life (lesson 5).
Learning how to deconstruct disagreements (lesson 6) and
How to resolve conflicts in real life and on social media (lesson 7),
Will help you to further handle the ups and downs of life.
Understanding the importance of navigating and managing social media (lesson 8),
You received instructions on how to seek wisdom and learn from your mistakes (lesson 9).
That results in your creating and maintaining healthy living and positive support systems (lesson 10).

You now have the tools and strategies to establish **YOUR** real living standards.
You are equipped to successfully navigate growing through adolescence, college, and adulthood.
In other words, LIFE.

Congratulations!!!!

Now go forth and conquer your world!!

CERTIFICATE OF ACHIEVEMENT

is presented to

for completion of

G.I.R.L.S. Program

Deirdre Shelton
_____
G.I.R.L.S Founder

_____
Facilitator

_____
Date

NOTES

Made in the USA
Monee, IL
07 March 2023

29247661R00093